DK EYEWITNESS

T0017174

TOP 10
CANCÚN AND
THE YUCATÁN

Top 10 Cancún and the Yucatán Highlights

The Top 10 of Everything

Welcome to Cancún
and the Yucatán 5

Exploring Cancún
and the Yucatán 6

Cancún and the
Yucatán Highlights 10

Cancún..12

Cozumel 14

Playa del Carmen 16

Isla Mujeres................................20

Tulum..22

Sian Ka'an Biosphere
Reserve.....................................26

Chichén Itzá................................28

Mérida..32

Uxmal 34

Campeche 38

Moments in History 42

Popular Mayan Sites..................44

Churches 46

Spanish-era Towns.....................48

Beaches..50

Diving Reefs 52

Eco-Parks and Theme Parks......54

Wildlife Reserves 56

Cenotes and Caves 58

Sports and Activities..................60

Off the Beaten Path 62

Children's Attractions................64

Nightspots...................................66

Dishes of the Yucatán 68

Restaurants.................................70

Cancún and the Yucatán
for Free......................................72

Festivals.......................................74

CONTENTS

Cancún and the Yucatán Area by Area

Cancún and the North **78**

Cozumel and the South **90**

The Central Heartland **100**

The West **108**

Streetsmart

Getting Around **118**

Practical Information **120**

Places to Stay **126**

General Index **134**

Acknowledgments **140**

Phrase Book **142**

Within each Top 10 list in this book, no hierarchy of quality or popularity is implied. All 10 are, in the editor's opinion, of roughly equal merit.

Throughout this book, floors are referred to in accordance with American usage; i.e., the "first floor" is at ground level.

Title page, front cover and spine *Ruins of the temple of Ixchel at the beach of Isla Mujeres* ***Back cover, clockwise from top left*** *Hawksbill turtle in Cozumel; street in Mérida; Castillo de Kukulcán pyramid; the temple of Ixchel; palm tree-shaded beach*

The rapid rate at which the world is changing is constantly keeping the DK Eyewitness team on our toes. While we've worked hard to ensure that this edition of Cancún and the Yucatán is accurate and up-to-date, we know that opening hours alter, standards shift, prices fluctuate, places close and new ones pop up in their stead. So, if you notice we've got something wrong or left something out, we want to hear about it. Please get in touch at **travelguides@dk.com**

Welcome to
Cancún and the Yucatán

Beautiful Caribbean beaches and epic Mayan sites. Stunning colonial cities and pristine diving reefs. Tropical islands and nature reserves rich with wildlife. Mouthwatering cuisine and vibrant nightlife. Whatever strikes your fancy, this region has something for everyone. With DK Eyewitness Top 10 Cancún and the Yucatán, it's yours to explore.

Set between the Caribbean Sea and the Gulf of Mexico, the Yucatán Peninsula is one of the country's most popular tourist destinations. Its focal point is **Cancún**, a lively mega-resort with a dazzling array of hotels, restaurants, bars, clubs, stores, and activities. South of Cancún, the Mayan Riviera stretches from mellow **Puerto Morelos** and hip **Playa del Carmen** to picturesque **Tulum**, with its palm-fringed beach overlooked by a clifftop Mayan temple. Beyond lie the wildlife paradise of **Sian Ka'an** and the diving haven of **Cozumel** island.

Inland are some of the world's finest archaeological sites, notably the dramatic Mayan sites of **Chichén Itzá** and **Uxmal**. The region has also been heavily influenced by the Spanish: **Mérida** is one of the most delightful cities in Mexico, filled with Moorish-style townhouses, palm-shaded patios, colonnaded squares, and whitewashed churches.

Whether you're visiting for a weekend or a week, our Top 10 guide brings together the best of everything the region has to offer, from the Caribbean hideaway of **Isla Mujeres** to the historic walled town of **Campeche** on the Gulf of Mexico. The guide has useful tips throughout, from seeking out what's free to places off the beaten path, plus six easy-to-follow itineraries designed to tie together a clutch of sights in a short space of time. Add inspiring photography and detailed maps, and you've got the essential pocket-sized travel companion. **Enjoy the book, and enjoy Cancún and the Yucatán.**

Clockwise from top: Isla Mujeres beach, Cancún's Museo Subacuático de Arte, brightly painted buildings in Campeche, Chichén Itzá's great pyramid, angelfish at the Sian Ka'an Biosphere Reserve, beach at Playa del Carmen, traditional Mexican ceramics at a street stall

Exploring Cancún and the Yucatán

This diverse region has a fabulous range of attractions, and deciding where to visit and what to do can be a challenge. However long your stay, you'll want to make the most of your time, and these two sightseeing itineraries will help you get the very best out of your visit to Cancún and the Yucatán.

Playa del Carmen's lively and colorful street life is just one of its many attractions.

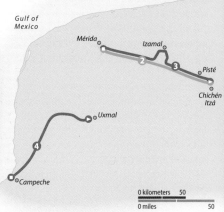

The beach at Tulum is overlooked by the spectacular site of a great Mayan temple.

Two Days in Cancún and the Yucatán

Day ❶
MORNING
Start the day on the beach in **Cancún** (see pp12–13), before paying a visit to the spectacular Museo Subacuático de Arte or the Gran Museo del Mundo Maya. Afterwards grab a seafood lunch at **La Habichuela** (see p87).

AFTERNOON
Head down the coast to **Playa del Carmen** (see pp16–17) for a stroll down Quinta Avenida, followed by a visit to the **Xcaret** (see pp18–19) eco-park or a lounge at a beach club such as **INTI Beach** (see p86). Or head further south to **Tulum** (see pp22–3), where you can explore the Mayan sites (see p91) before having dinner at **Hartwood** (see p70).

Day ❷
MORNING
Set off early for **Chichén Itzá** (see pp28–31), where you can explore the Castillo de Kukulcán, the Great Ball Court and the Temple of the Warriors.

AFTERNOON
Drive to **Mérida** (see pp32–3) and lunch at **El Marlín Azul** (see p115). Spend the the afternoon in the historic center, before taking advantage of the city's free evening entertainment (see p72).

Four Days in Cancún and the Yucatán

Day ❶
MORNING
Start in **Cancún** (see pp12–13) – head to the beach, shop and look round the Gran Museo del Mundo Maya, or visit the Museo Subacuático de Arte.

Chichén Itzá, one of the most magnificent Mayan complexes, is dominated by the dramatic stepped pyramid known as the Castillo de Kukulcán.

Key

━━ Two-day itinerary
━━ Four-day itinerary

Isla Mujeres
FERRY
Cancún
Gran Museo del Mundo Maya
Museo Subacuático de Arte
①
Playa del Carmen
Xcaret
FLIGHT
①
Isla de Cozumel
Tulum
②
Hartwood
Sian Ka'an Biosphere Reserve
Caribbean Sea

Day ❸

MORNING

Start early for the two-hour drive from either **Playa** (see pp16–17) or **Tulum** (see pp22–3) to **Chichén Itzá** (see pp28–31). Have lunch in Pisté at **Las Mestizas** (see p107).

AFTERNOON

Head west to **Mérida** (see pp32–3), calling in on the way at the craft workshops of **Izamal** (see p105). Spend the rest of the day exploring Mérida's historic center, before dinner at **La Chaya Maya** (see p115).

Day ❹

MORNING

Set off for the evocative Mayan sites of **Uxmal** (see pp34–7) before getting lunch at **Hacienda Uxmal** (see p115), set just opposite the sites.

AFTERNOON

Head to **Campeche** (see pp38–9) where you can explore the walled old town or stroll along the Malecón at sunset. End your day with dinner at **La Pigua** (see p115).

AFTERNOON

After lunch take the ferry over to **Isla Mujeres** (see pp20–21) or fly down to **Cozumel** (see pp14–15) – both islands are excellent for scuba diving.

Day ❷

MORNING

Return by ferry to the mainland, then head south along the coast to **Playa del Carmen** (see pp16–17).

AFTERNOON

After lunch, visit the **Xcaret** eco-park (see pp18–19), before starting your night out at **Abolengo** (see p86). Alternatively, continue further south to **Tulum** (see pp22–3) where you can visit the Mayan sites (see p91). After that, head to the **Sian Ka'an Biosphere Reserve** (see pp26–7). Take a guided tour of its highlights before making your way back to Tulum.

The city walls of Campeche hold a preserved colonial Spanish city.

Top 10 Cancún and the Yucatán Highlights

The magnificent Castillo de Kukulcán pyramid at Chichén Itzá

Cancún and the
  Yucatán Highlights   10

Cancún   12

Cozumel   14

Playa del Carmen   16

Isla Mujeres   20

Tulum   22

Sian Ka'an
  Biosphere Reserve   26

Chichén Itzá   28

Mérida   32

Uxmal   34

Campeche   38

⓾ Cancún and the Yucatán Highlights

The Yucatán Peninsula charts the history of Mexico, from ancient Mayan civilizations to the Spanish era and on to the arrival of tourism. Today, the region is famed for its ancient sights, Mayan villages and beautiful beaches.

① Cancún
Mexico's biggest resort has miles of white-sand beaches, lavish hotels, every kind of restaurant, and attractions from water parks to giant nightclubs (see pp12–13).

Cozumel ②
The divers' favorite, with over 20 coral reefs to delight first-time snorkelers and experienced divers alike (see pp14–15).

③ Playa del Carmen
The trendiest spot on the Riviera Maya, Playa is on a more small-town scale than Cancún, with superb swimming and snorkeling, and an ever-buzzing nightlife (see pp16–19).

Isla Mujeres ④
This stunning Caribbean island has a beachcomber style, and is surrounded by superb diving reefs (see pp20–21).

⑤ Tulum
One of the most spectacular Mayan sites perches on a crag overlooking palm-lined sands and relaxed cabaña hotels (see pp22–3).

Map labels:
Dzilam de Bravo, Telchac, Progreso, Dzidzantun, Gulf of Mexico, Sisal, Conkal, Motul, Hunucmá, Mérida ⑧, Izan, Uman, Acanceh, Celestún, Kantunil, Maxcanú, Telchaquillo, Tekit, Yaxcab, Muna, Uxmal ⑨, Ticul, Chunhuas, Oxkutzcab, Tekax, Pet, Tenabo, Santa Rosa, ⑩ Campeche, Nohalal, Hopelchen, Nohyaxché, Haltunchen, Dzibalchen

6 Sian Ka'an Biosphere Reserve

This almost uninhabited expanse of lakes, reefs, lagoon, mangroves, and forest is home to jaguars, monkeys, and millions of birds and rare plants *(see pp26–7)*.

7 Chichén Itzá

The most awe-inspiring of all Mayan cities, Chichén has massive pyramids looming over huge plazas, intricately aligned with the movements of the sun and stars *(see pp28–31)*.

8 Mérida

Atmospheric squares, shady patios, whitewashed facades, and characterful markets make this beautiful and culturally rich city a must-visit on any tour of the region *(see pp32–3)*.

9 Uxmal

The pyramids, palaces, and quadrangles of this dramatic city have a particular elegance and beauty, and are regarded by many as the pinnacle of Mayan architecture *(see pp34–7)*.

10 Campeche

This city is a remarkable survivor from the Spanish era. It includes an old section ringed by ramparts and bastions, and a superb museum of Mayan relics housed in an ancient fortress *(see pp38–9)*.

TOP 10 ⭐ Cancún

Just a dot on the map before 1970, Cancún is now the biggest resort in the Caribbean. Its Hotel Zone occupies a huge, narrow sand spit shaped like a giant "7." Over on the mainland lies the town of Ciudad Cancún, also known as Downtown. All along Boulevard Kukulcán are hotels, shopping malls, restaurants, and visitor attractions, including some excellent museums and atmospheric Mayan sites.

The Beach ①

Cancún's greatest glory is made up of fine white silicate sand **(right)** that is soft and some-how always cool despite the warmth of the sun. There are several public access points from Boulevard Kukulcán. The north side of the "7" is best for swim-ming; the eastern beaches have more crashing waves.

③ Avenida Tulum and Downtown

The hub of the more Mexican part of Ciudad Cancún is tree-lined Avenida Tulum. It's a good spot for a stroll, and its cafés and restau-rants are more tranquil than those by the beach.

⑤ Gran Museo del Mundo Maya

This beautiful museum is dedicated to the ancient Mayan civilization. Right next to the striking mod-ern building that houses it is an archaeological site called San Miguelito with plenty to explore.

② Shopping Areas

Cancún is a shopaholic's heaven, where visitors will find everything from Mexican souvenirs in the markets of Downtown to international fashion in the vast, gleaming malls of the Hotel Zone, such as the exclusive water-side development of La Isla **(above)**.

④ Museo Subacuático de Arte

Over 500 statues **(below)**, created by British sculptor Jason deCaires Taylor, are viewed via scuba-diving, snorkelling, or on a glass-bottomed boat.

7 El Rey Site

These structures (left) were part of a city that was prominent in the last centuries of Mayan civilization, just before the Spanish invasion. Close to the site is a re-creation of a Mayan village, where visitors can get an insight into the Mayan way of life, including traditional cooking styles.

A GROWING RESORT

The Dreams hotel at the tip of Punta Cancún is where Cancún started back in 1971, when it opened as the first hotel on the island. The rest of the "7" was then empty except for trees, dunes, and a very few beach houses and fishing lodges. Since then, Cancún has acquired over 32,000 hotel rooms.

9 Laguna Nichupté

The placid lagoon enclosed by Cancún Island offers more tranquility than the ocean, and is a favorite place for watersports. To the west are mangroves and jungle.

Map of Cancún

6 Ventura Park

This water park (see p64) has slides and rides of all sizes for all ages, a snorkeling pool with stingrays and (harmless) sharks, and even bungee-jumping.

8 El Meco Site

Near the Isla Mujeres ferry ports, the city of El Meco dates back to 300 CE. An impressive pyramid and the remains of an opulent Mayan palace can be seen.

NEED TO KNOW

MAP H2 & R2–S2

Visitor Info: kiosks inside Town Hall; (998) 881 9000; www.caribemexicano.travel

El Rey Site: open 9am–4:30pm daily; adm $3.50

El Meco Site: open 8am–4pm daily; adm $3.50

Gran Museo del Mundo Maya: Blvd Kukulcán, km

16.5; (998) 885 3842; open 9am–6pm Tue–Sun; adm $5

Museo Subacuático de Arte: Blvd Kukulcán, km 15.3; (998) 848 8312; open 9am–5pm daily; adm varies

■ Buses R-1, R-2, R-15 run from Avenida Tulum to the Hotel Zone (24 hours).

■ Try the restaurants at Mercado 28 (Downtown).

10 Nighttime Cancún

Cancún's nightlife is most concentrated in the "Corazón" but it extends all the way to Ciudad Cancún. A non-stop party atmosphere is maintained in clubs varying from Mexican traditional to modern cool.

🔟 ⭐ Cozumel

The island of Cozumel was the first part of the Yucatán to become popular with visitors from abroad after the famous oceanographer Jacques Cousteau came here in the 1950s. One of the world's largest coral reef systems, Cozumel was declared by Cousteau to be one of the finest diving areas in the world. The offshore reef is full of life and a dazzling array of colors. Onshore, Cozumel has an easygoing atmosphere, ideal for families.

1 Laguna Chankanaab

Created around a natural coral lagoon (see p54), this glorious park **(below)** includes a botanical garden, a pretty beach, and reefs that are ideal for novice divers.

4 San Miguel

Cozumel's only town has a laid-back street life centered on the waterfront (Malecón) and Plaza Cozumel **(right)**. The island's Punta Langosta cruise terminal (see p96) is located here.

2 North Beach Hotel Zone

The island's biggest upscale hotel cluster is situated along a shaded boulevard north of town. Hotels and resorts line a row of intimate beaches. Pools, watersports, and every comfort are on hand, and there are fine views across the channel to the Yucatán mainland from most hotel rooms.

3 Playa Mia and Playa San Francisco

These are two of Cozumel's best beaches, with the option to rent water tricycles and kayaks.

5 Punta Santa Cecilia and Chen Río

The east side of the island is more rugged and windblown than the west, with rocky, empty beaches and crashing surf that can be dangerous to swim in. At Punta Santa Cecilia there's a lonely beach bar, Mezcalito's, which has great views, while Chen Río has a lovely sheltered beach and a seafood restaurant idyllically situated right on the shore.

Map of Cozumel

6 Museo de Cozumel

San Miguel's charming waterfront museum tells the story of Mayan Cozumel, the arrival of the Spaniards, and the pirate era. It has a lovely rooftop café (see p98).

Paraíso Reef 7

Shallow and close to the shore, this is a favorite reef for snorkeling, scuba courses, and easy diving by day and night. Parrotfish **(right)** are commonly sighted.

MAYAN COZUMEL

As a shrine to Ixchel, goddess of fertility, Cozumel was one of the most important places of pilgrimage in the Yucatán in the centuries just before the Spanish invasion (see p42). A visit here was seen as especially important for childless women, though everyone in Mayan Yucatán tried to make the trip at least once in their lives.

NEED TO KNOW

MAP H3–4 & R5–6

Visitor Info: (987) 869 0212; www.caribemexicano.travel/isla-cozumel

Laguna Chankanaab: (987) 872 1522; open 8am–4pm Mon–Sat; adm $26, $19 under 12s, under 4s free; snorkel hire extra; www.cozumelparks.com/parque-chankanaab

San Gervasio Site: open 8am–5pm daily; adm $5; under 10s free

Punta Sur Eco Beach Park: open 9am–5pm Mon–Sat; adm $19, $13 under 12s; under 4s free

Museo de Cozumel: open 9am–5pm Tue–Sun; adm $9; www.cozumelparks.com/en/cozumel-museum

Cozumel Parks: (987) 872 1522; www.cozumelparks.com

■ Waters off Cozumel are clear and reefs are close to the surface. You can often see a lot just by snorkeling or free-diving.

■ The best places to eat on the island are the restaurants along the wild east coast of Cozumel.

8 Palancar Reef

The most famous of Cozumel's reefs, the Palancar Reef has fabulous coral canyons and red and blue caves. The waters are full of vibrant creatures, including the luminous angelfish.

9 San Gervasio Site

Cozumel's Mayan capital was one of the richest religious and trading cities in pre-Conquest Yucatán. The layout of its pyramids and small palaces gives a strong impression of life in a Mayan community.

10 Punta Sur Eco Beach Park

A wildly diverse nature reserve **(left)** with turtle-nesting beaches, huge mangroves and lagoons that are home to crocodiles and flamingos, and a snorkeling area. There's also a lighthouse and a tiny Mayan temple.

TOP 10 ⭐ Playa del Carmen

If you prefer a beachtown atmosphere to the long hotel strip of Cancún, this is the ideal choice on the Mayan Riviera. A tiny fishing village with sand streets in the 1980s, and a backpackers' hangout in the early 1990s, Playa has blossomed into a fun town with an energetic beach scene and nightlife.

1 Quinta Avenida
Stretching north from the town plaza, "Fifth Avenue" is Playa's main drag, for daytime shopping and nighttime promenading – a multi-colored array of shops, cafés, hotels, clubs, and restaurants.

3 Chunzubul Beach
Playa's best snorkeling spot is found along the beautiful Chunuzbul reef, just off the beach by the same name. There are also nudist beaches along this stretch of coast.

5 Town Beach
At the center of the action by day is the main beach **(below)**, with beautiful soft, white Yucatán sand and plenty of shoreline cafés. Beach volleyball is something of a specialty.

2 Playacar
This very smartly landscaped development **(below)** shows a different side of Playa. It encompasses resort hotels, winding lanes of luxury villas, an aviary, Mayan sites, beach clubs, restaurants, and a championship standard golf course *(see p60)*.

4 INTI Beach
This amazing spot has a more relaxed ambience than some of the area's see-and-be-seen clubs, which is precisely why many visitors love it. The club's restaurant on the beach is a top draw.

Map of Playa del Carmen

CALLE 46
CALLE 38
AVENIDA 30
AVENIDA 10
CALLE 26
AVE CONSTITUYENTES
CALLE 12
AVENIDA 25
AVENIDA 15
AVENIDA 5
CALLE 1
Caribbean Sea
PASEO COBA
Playacar
PASEO XAMAN-HA
➏ 4 miles (6 km)

➌
➍
➊
➑
➎
➒
➓
➋

SLEEP ALL NIGHT, PARTY ALL DAY

Playa del Carmen isn't known as party central without reason – you really can party all night here. However, party-goers also have the opportunity to party all day. Establishments such as the Coralina Daylight Club *(see p85)* make use of their warm and sandy locations to attract patrons while the sun is still up.

8 Nighttime Playa

After dark the Quinta buzzes with crowds strolling, dining, and bar-hopping. With mariachi bands **(above)** in some places and techno DJs in others, there's plenty of variety. The heart of the action is the junction of the Quinta and Calle 12.

9 Xaman-Ha Aviary

The aviary located within Playacar contains a fine collection of toucans, parrots, flamingos, and over 60 other bird species in a lush green setting that seems almost like real jungle. This is a very easy way for visitors to see some of the Yucatán's rarer birds without trekking into the forest.

10 Xaman-Ha Mayan Site

Playa shares its ground with the site of a Mayan settlement known as Xaman-Ha **(below)**. Several temples survive, with most scattered around the Playacar area.

6 Xcaret

Created around a natural lagoon 4 miles (6 km) south of Playa, this "eco-park" *(see pp18–19)* is bursting with flora, fauna, and sea life.

7 Playa's Hip Hotels

Playa is well known for its stylish small hotels, such as Deseo. Discreetly spectacular and with lovely pools, they showcase contemporary style and elegance.

NEED TO KNOW

MAP H3 & Q4

Visitor Info: Av 20 and 1ª Sur; (984) 873 0242; open 9am–8:30pm Mon–Fri (until 5pm Sat & Sun); www.caribe mexicano.travel

Xcaret: **MAP G3 & Q4**; open 8:30am–10:30pm; tours daily from Cancún and Playa del Mar; adm $120–200, $90; children 5–11 (under 5s free); www.xcaret.com

■ Snorkels are expensive to rent or buy in Playa.

■ For good traditional Mexican food at lower prices, eat away from the Quinta. Along Calle 4 there are several very enjoyable, low-key restaurants that serve up bargain seafood, such as the terrace-restaurant Las Brisas *(see p87)*.

TOP 10 Playa del Carmen: Xcaret

Visitors going snorkeling at La Caleta Cove inlet

1 La Caleta Cove and Blue Lagoon

Both of these are fine places for easy swimming. La Caleta ("the Inlet") was the main harbor of Mayan Polé and is now a favorite snorkeling spot, with coral and tropical fish just below the surface. The Blue Lagoon is a big, ultra-relaxing clearwater pool behind the beach, with islands of thick vegetation to explore.

2 Hacienda Henequenera

Henequén, a fiber derived from the agave plant, was a major industry in the Yucatán during the colonial period. This 19th-century mansion takes visitors back in time to learn more about this important part of Yucatecan history.

Quetzal, Aviary

3 Sea Trek

A fabulous guided walk – not swim – right along the seabed, using simple breathing apparatus and weights to prevent you from floating upwards. You don't need to be a great swimmer to enjoy this, and on the way you see all kinds of wonderful sea life from below.

4 Butterfly Garden

One of the most spectacular parts of Xcaret, the *mariposario* is the largest butterfly garden in the world, partly hidden in a steep ravine beneath a giant net of a roof. Bursting with all kinds of exuberant tropical flowers and plants, the garden is alive with an astonishing variety of colorful butterflies. Mornings are the best time to visit.

5 Aviary and Zoo

Animal attractions are spread all around the park. Among the birds on view – all of which are native to the Yucatán – are toucans, cute aracaris or "little toucans," bright green parrots, and the very rare quetzal, whose tail feathers were used in Mayan headdresses. Animals here include spider monkeys, bats, and pumas.

6 Turtle Pools

Near La Caleta, you will have the chance to see different kinds of sea turtles – leatherbacks, hawksbills,

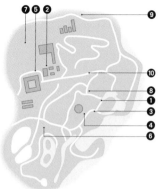

Map of Playa del Carmen: Xcaret

8 Forest Trail and Orchid Greenhouse

A well-signposted trail helps you to explore many other parts of the park, through lush natural forest and passing further attractions, such as beehives, animal enclosures, a mushroom farm, and a wonderful greenhouse with more than 100 magnificent varieties of rare orchid. You can also explore a longer, guided trail on horseback.

and loggerheads – in every stage of life, from tiny newborns to grumpy-faced ancients with beautiful shells over 3 ft (1 m) long. The pools are part of a repopulation program to preserve this endangered species, with turtles born here being released into the sea at 15 months. Visitors must maintain a safe distance while turtle-watching.

7 Mayan Village and Ball Court

Reached via a series of atmospheric passageways, the Mayan Village tries to re-create some of the life of the ancient Mayan world. This includes a reconstruction of a Mayan ball court, where a modern interpretation of the mysterious, long-lost ball game *(see p31)* is played daily. There's also a great museum by the park entrance.

Ball court at the Mayan Village

Snorkelers in the Underground River

9 Underground Snorkeling River

This clear, winding, turquoise stream allows visitors to swim and snorkel all the way through the park and the Mayan Village to the beach, via rocky canyons, pools, and caverns lit by shafts of daylight.

10 Live Show

Presented nightly, this is a spectacular mix of entertainment spread all around the village and theater. It begins with "ancient Mayan" rituals, mariachis, and vibrant performances of folk music and dances from all over Mexico, and goes on to a *charrería*, or Mexican rodeo.

TOP 10 ⭐ Isla Mujeres

Site of the first Spanish landing in Mexico in 1517, the "Island of Women" takes its name from the idols of the goddess Ixchel found here. Though close to Cancún, the island has a quite different, relaxed atmosphere, and has long been a backpackers' favorite. It also has excellent diving and fishing opportunities.

Colorful boats moored at the beachside dock at Isla Mujeres

1 Playa Norte
This beach **(below)** at the northern tip of the town is where many Isla visitors spend their days, with laid-back beach bars for refreshment breaks. With pure white sand and calm turquoise waters, it's excellent for tranquil swimming.

4 Playa Secreto
To the northeast of Isla town, this "secret" beach is in a sheltered inlet that's even more shallow and placid than Playa Norte.

5 Women's Beading Cooperative
Nearly 60 women are working members of this cooperative and earn a living by making jewelry. Visitors are welcome.

2 Sleeping Sharks Cave
An underground river meets the sea at this cave, and sharks come to bask, trancelike, in the mixture of fresh and salt water. A must-see for experienced divers; keep a safe distance from the sharks.

3 Isla Town
Isla's only town still has the look of a Caribbean fishing village **(right)**, with narrow, sandy streets and brightly painted wooden houses. There are plenty of cafés and souvenir shops, and few cars.

6 Manchones Reef

Isla Mujeres' favorite reef for scuba courses and easy diving. Only about 30–40 ft (10–12 m) deep, the waters are safe and have plenty of colorful coral and fish to observe.

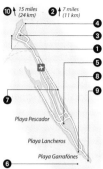

Map of Isla Mujeres

9 Parque Escultórico Punta Sur

The southern tip of the island has been transformed into a sculpture park with striking modern artworks spread around the windblown headland and lighthouse.

10 Isla Contoy

An uninhabited island about 18 miles (29 km) north of Isla Mujeres, Contoy **(right)** is an important seabird reserve for pelicans, cormorants, frigate birds, spoonbills, and others. Day trips are run by companies on Isla.

THE LAFITTES

Isla's most famous residents were the 19th-century Louisiana-born brothers Jean and Pierre Lafitte, considered the last infamous Caribbean pirates. Sailing south after falling out with the US government, they built a stronghold on the Isla lagoon, but were attacked by the Spanish Navy in 1821. Both badly wounded, they escaped in a boat. Pierre is thought to have died in Dzilam Bravo on the mainland; Jean's fate remains a mystery.

7 Guadalupe Chapel

A simple and humble church, the Guadalupe Chapel looks out onto the sea and offers a very inspiring view. There's a small gift shop on site, which sells handmade jewelry. The church also acts as a venue for events such as *quinceañeras* (a young girl's coming-of-age celebration) and weddings.

8 El Garrafón

This nature park and snorkeling center is created around a natural, shallow pool. There are restaurants, equipment rental, and swimming and snorkeling opportunities in the rock pool, offshore reefs, or in the swimming pool.

NEED TO KNOW
MAP H2, S1 & L1–2

Visitor Info: Av Rueda Medina 130, to the left from the ferry quay; open 9am–4pm Mon–Fri; www.caribemexicano.travel

Guadalupe Chapel: Av Perimetral Oriente; (998) 705 9911; open 8am Sun for Mass

Women's Beading Cooperative: open 9am–5pm Mon–Sat, 10am–3pm Sun

Parque Garrafón: (01) 866 393 5158; open 9am–5:30pm daily; adm $89–$199; www.garrafon.com

Parque Escultórico Punta Sur: open 10am–6pm daily; adm $6

■ The slow ferry from Puerto Juárez to Isla is the cheapest and nicest ride.

■ Rent a golf cart, scooter, or bike to see the island.

■ Buy food for a picnic at Isla Town before touring the island.

★ Tulum

One of the Yucatán's most beautiful places, Tulum offers its visitors a breathtaking combination of spectacular Mayan sites and miles of superb, palm-fringed beaches. Nearby, too, is the finest cave-diving area in the world. This is the most popular destination in the Yucatán for renting cabañas – simple rooms in palm-roofed cabins set right by the beach within earshot of the waves.

1 Tulum Site
Mayan Tulum was a walled town and prosperous trading community when the Spaniards arrived in the 1520s. The site **(right)** includes a recognizable main street, the House of the Columns, and the Palace of the Halach Uinic.

2 Tulum Pueblo
A rambling place spread out along the main highway, Tulum village was almost 100 per cent Mayan, but it now has a bank, bus terminus, cafés, small hotels, and backpacker services.

3 Playa Paraíso
Set against a backdrop of the iconic El Castillo, Paradise Beach is widely considered as one of the best beaches in Mexico. It has clean sand and clear Caribbean waters, and is a must-visit for visitors to Tulum.

4 Tankah Natural Park
Part of Tankah Bay, the park offers jeep, zip-line, and canoe rides through lush forests, as well as the opportunity to visit a Mayan village located within the park.

5 Secluded Heaven
Along a stretch of beach south of the T-junction in the road is a wide choice of beach cabins, from sand-floor huts to luxurious cabañas, most of them secluded. Few have electricity and are lit only by candles at night.

6 Aktun-Ha Cenote
An enjoyable cenote for swimming **(left)**, with a broad, peaceful pool that runs into a dark and mysterious cave system. As you swim, you'll see many shoals of tiny fish.

8 Xel-Ha

This coral inlet **(left)** has been landscaped as a snorkel park, plus forest trail and beach. It has plenty of colorful fish and is a great place for children. Across the highway is the site of a Mayan city.

9 Gran Cenote

Along the road toward Cobá from Tulum are several accessible cenotes in which visitors can take a cooling dip. Surrounded by rock columns and beautiful flowers, and leading into into a wide, arching cavern, the Gran Cenote is one of the area's most appealing for swimmers and snorkelers.

CENOTES

Some 65 million years ago an asteroid struck the Yucatán Peninsula, an event that helped to precipitate the extinction of the dinosaurs. The impact also formed vast networks of limestone caves, subterranean rivers, and cenotes, natural sinkholes fed by springs. Swimming or diving in these cenotes, which vary from tiny wells to cathedral-like caverns, is an unforgettable experience. Cave-diving trips are offered across the Tulum area.

10 El Castillo

The most impressive of the Mayan buildings is the great temple **(above)**. A flaming beacon lit at the top of the temple was once visible for miles.

Map of Tulum

7 Dos Ojos Cenote

This is the entrance to the world's longest known underwater cave system, which stretches over 350 miles (563 km).

NEED TO KNOW
MAP G4 & P6

Visitor Info: www.caribemexi cano.travel/riviera-maya; www.inah.gob.mx

Gran Cenote and Aktun–Ha Cenote: open 9am–5pm daily; adm $12

Xel-Ha: open 8:30am–6pm daily; adm $90, children $65; under 4s free; www.xelha.com

Tulum Site: open 8am–5pm daily; adm $5; www.inah. gob.mx/zonas/99-zona-arqueologica-de-tulum

Tankah Natural Park: open 9am–5pm daily; adm $40–50; www.tankah.com.mx

Dos Ojos Cenote: tours 8am–5pm daily; adm per activity; www.cenote dosojos.com

■ In peak season the cheaper beach cabañas are often booked up by 10am each day.

■ Diamante-K cabañas, north of the T-junction, have a vegetarian café and juice bar, open to non-residents.

Following pages Visitors taking pictures near the beautiful Ik Kil Cenote at Chichén Itzá

TOP 10 ⭐ Sian Ka'an Biosphere Reserve

The jungle and wetlands of Sian Ka'an (Mayan for "where the sky is born") contrast strikingly with the resorts of the Mayan Riviera. Extending south from Tulum around Ascension Bay and encompassing lagoons, reefs, lakes, mangroves, and forests, the area is virtually uninhabited and contains a dazzling variety of animal and plant life.

Muyil Site ①
The ancient Mayan city of Muyil lies just outside the reserve. An ancient city possibly allied to Cobá *(see p92)*, it has an unusual great pyramid **(right)** with a multiroomed building at its top. Beside the site, a path leads to Lake Chunyaxché.

② Boca Paila
Set on a glorious lagoon, the Boca Paila Fishing Lodge is a favorite among serious fishers. This is also where Sian Ka'an tours switch from vans to boats.

③ Punta Allen
It is said that this lobster-fishing village, with its sandy streets, big beach, and handful of places to eat and stay, was founded by Blackbeard, whose ship was called *The Allen*.

④ Lake Chunyaxché
Sian Ka'an has many lakes that, like all those in the Yucatán, are fed by underground streams. The channels from the lagoon into the lake have points where the sea and lake waters meet, bringing together a teeming mix of plant life and fish.

⑥ Lake Islands
There are more than 20 Mayan sites within the reserve, many of them small temples sited on islands in the lakes. It is thought that these isolated lake island temples were probably places of pilgrimage, visited in order to perform special rituals.

⑤ Animals
Sian Ka'an is home to every kind of wild cat found in Mexico and Central America, including ocelots and pumas, as well as anteaters, manatees, and tapirs. However, you're most likely to see raccoons, spider monkeys, bush pigs, iguanas, and gray foxes **(left)**.

7 Ascension Bay Bonefishing Flats

These shallows are among the best flyfishing areas in the world, above all for bonefish. Lodges along the road, and Punta Allen's guesthouses, offer trips to them.

Map of the Sian Ka'an Biosphere Reserve

CHECHEN AND CHAKAH

The toxicity of the small chechen tree can make people numb and dizzy by its aroma alone. But if local Maya ever rub against the tree's leaves, they know they have only to look around for a nearby chakah bush to find the natural antidote to the chechen's poison.

9 Native and Migratory Birds

Nearly 350 bird species have been logged as native to the Sian Ka'an Biosphere Reserve, and around a million migratory birds visit each year from North America. Among those easiest for visitors to see are ibises, egrets, orioles, storks, American herons, and flamingos **(right)**.

10 Ben-Ha Cenote

By the warden's lodge at the reserve's entrance, a path leads to a clear, cool cenote, where you can swim among reeds and forest trees.

8 Mangroves and Forest

A mix of salt and fresh water at Sian Ka'an provides the ideal conditions for mangroves **(right)**. Further inland are large expanses of rain forest and grasslands.

NEED TO KNOW

MAP F5–6 ■ Entry to the reserve is $5 per person, but to see the best of the wildlife it is worth joining an eco-friendly tour

Sian Ka'an Tours, Tulum: (984) 871 2202; tours cost from around $90 and above per person (prices vary with tours); www.siankaantours.org

■ The operator listed above sometimes offers specialist tours, such as snorkeling, bird-watching, or looking for crocodiles at night.

■ Tours tend to include refreshments (drinks and sandwiches usually), but if you are traveling independently, eat or buy food at Punta Allen.

■ Be sure to wear sensible footwear with sturdy soles when visiting the reserve.

TOP 10 ⭐ Chichén Itzá

Built to a scale that seems to be from another world, Chichén, one of the new seven wonders of the world, has some of the largest buildings of the ancient Mayan cities. It had a port near Río Lagartos and grew rich from trading. With a large population, it became the most powerful city in the whole of the Yucatán in the last centuries of the Classic Mayan era (750–900 CE), defeating Cobá, Izamal, and others in war. A visit to this site is not to be missed.

2 Nunnery
The Spaniards thought this group of buildings was a nunnery, but experts now believe it formed the main residential and administrative area for Chichén's lords in the city's first years. The buildings are covered in a wealth of spectacular carvings.

5 High Priest's Grave
This pyramid is inscribed with the date of its completion: June 20 842. It is named for a tomb excavated at its foot, which cannot be visited.

1 Observatory
The observatory (above) is also called El Caracol ("snail") for its odd round shape. Three slots in its top level point due south and toward the setting sun and moon on the spring and fall equinoxes.

3 Great Ball Court
Built in 864 CE, this is the biggest ancient ball court (see p31) in Mexico. It has exceptional carvings and remarkably good acoustics.

6 Castillo de Kukulcán
It is no longer possible to climb this awesome pyramid (below), which encloses an older one, that is accessed from the top of the Castillo. Carvings, panels, levels, and the 365 steps are symbols of the intricate Mayan calendar.

4 Sound and Light Show
Presented nightly, the show features an imagined history of Chichén Itzá, while the main temples are dramatically lit in changing colors.

Map of Chichén Itzá

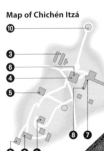

⓵ ⓶ ⓷ ⓸ ⓹ ⓺ ⓻ ⓼ ⓽ ⓾

On the spring equinox, the afternoon sun picks out the tails of the serpents lining the Castillo's north stairway and runs down to their heads just before sunset. On the autumn equinox, the reverse effect occurs. This "Descent of Kukulcán" symbolized the city's contact with the gods. Today, crowds flock to see the event.

7 Temple of the Warriors

The squat temple **(above)** opposite the Castillo was used in city rituals. In front of it are ranks of pillars, each intricately carved with portraits of important figures in the Chichén elite.

8 Court of the Thousand Columns

The forest of pillars around a giant quadrangle once supported wood and palm roofs. This was Chichén's main place for doing business: for buying, selling, and voicing disputes.

9 Old Chichén

Chichén Itzá once covered a much wider area than is seen at its monumental core. To the south is Chichén Viejo – a part-excavated site in the woods that is as old as the central plazas.

10 Sacred Cenote

Visited by Mayan pilgrims over centuries, the Sacred Cenote **(above)** *(see p23)*, has yielded up jewelry, sculptures, and bones of animals.

NEED TO KNOW
MAP E3

Open 8am–5pm daily
■ www.chichenitza.inah.gob.mx

Adm $5 (under 14s free)

Sound and Light Show: winter: 7pm daily, summer: 8pm daily; adm included in main entrance fee, but $2.50 extra for English, Italian, German, or French commentary on headphones; www.inah.gob.mx

■ To see Chichén at its best, stay nearby the night before and get to the site early, before the heat of the day and before the arrival of the large crowds from Cancún at about 11am.

■ The town of Pisté west of the site has several pleasant restaurants along its main street, such as Las Mestizas *(see p107)*, which have more charm than the visitor center at the site itself.

Chichén Itzá: The Carvings

1 Casa Colorada Inscriptions

These record that Chichén lords celebrated a ritual in September 869 to ensure the city's prosperity.

2 Chac-Masks of Las Monjas

The curling snout of the rain-god Chac is depicted repeatedly in rows at the Nunnery.

3 Platform of the Jaguars and Eagles

This small platform may have been used for rituals by the warrior Orders of the Jaguars and Eagles. Its carvings show these animals tearing open human victims to eat their hearts.

Platform of the Jaguars and Eagles

4 Chac Mool and Altar of the Red Jaguar

Reclining Chac Mool figures were fallen warriors delivering offerings to the gods, from food and jewels to the hearts of sacrificial victims. The Chac Mool in the temple of the Castillo lies before a painted stone jaguar throne.

5 Temple of the Jaguars

Carved panels in this temple connect the foundation of Chichén Itzá with First Mother and First Father, the creators of the world.

6 Ball Court Frieze

As defeated ball game players have their heads cut off, seven spurts of blood shoot from their necks and transform into vines and flowers.

Heads of Kukulcán at the Castillo

7 Heads of Kukulcán

The giant feathered serpents at the Castillo probably represented Vision Serpents *(see p43)* but they have also been associated with the central Mexican serpent-god Quetzalcóatl.

8 Tzompantli

Covered in carved skulls on all four sides, a low platform near the Ball Court was probably used to display the heads of sacrificial victims.

9 Warriors' Columns

A "picture gallery" of the men of Chichén. Most are of warriors in their battle regalia, but there are also some priests and bound captives.

10 Snails, Armadillos, Turtles, and Crabs

Placed between the Chac-heads on the Iglesia ("church") at the Nunnery, these animals represented the four spirits that held up the sky at the cardinal points (north, south, east, west) in Mayan mythology.

Map of Chichén Itzá's Carvings

THE BALL GAME

The ancient Mexican ball game can be traced back to before 1500 BCE. It features in Mayan myths such as the story of the hero-twins Hunahpu and Xbalanqué, who play the game with the Lords of Death for days and nights, defying the forces of destiny. There were ball courts in all Mayan cities. No one knows exactly how the game was played, but it is thought that there were two main forms. One was played by two or four players on the older, smaller courts, and the aim was to keep the ball from touching the ground and get it past your opponent(s) and out at the end of the court. The other form corresponded to much bigger courts, such as at Chichén Itzá, and was played by teams of seven who scored in big rings on either side of the court. In either style players could not touch the ball with hands or feet, but only with shoulders, chest and hips, so scoring was very hard. Games had great ritual significance, and sometimes, but not always, losing players were sacrificed to the gods.

The Ball Court
Ball courts were found in all the ancient cultures of Mexico and Central America. Though the style and size of the courts varied, they were always I-shaped, as in the Aztec codex illustration below. The game was viewed as symbolic of the cycle of life, and the court represented the world. While games had important religious significance, it is known that men also placed bets on the results.

TOP 10
ANCIENT MAYAN BALL COURTS

1 Monte Albán, Oaxaca
2 Palenque, Chiapas
3 Toniná, Chiapas
4 Uxmal, Yucatán
5 Chichén Itzá, Yucatán
6 Cobá, Quintana Roo
7 Kohunlich, Quintana Roo
8 Calakmul, southern Campeche
9 Tikal, Guatemala
10 Copán, Honduras

A carved stone ring was the hoop through which players had to shoot the ball. It was placed vertically, at 27 ft (8 m) high.

TOP 10 ⭐ Mérida

Founded in 1542 by the Spanish, Merida was built on the site of an ancient Mayan settlement. The city is the largest in the Yucatan, today Merida is known for its Moorish-style Spanish houses, tall 17th-century churches, and unhurried street life. It is also at the center of the Yucatán's distinctive culture, making it the best place to see and shop for traditional crafts and souvenirs.

1 Palacio del Gobernador

Set next to the cathedral, the elegant seat of the Yucatán state govern-ment was built in 1892 to replace a Spanish gov-ernors' palace. Its patios, open to the public, are decorated with striking murals by Fernando Castro Pacheco, telling the story of the Mayans.

4 Cathedral

Built between 1562 and 1598, this is the oldest cathedral on the American mainland (in the entire continent, only Santo Domingo in the Dominican Republic is older). Massive and monumental, it was built in the sober style of the Spanish Renaissance, with a soaring facade and relatively few deco-rative flourishes.

2 Museo Casa Montejo

The astonishing portico **(above)** of the first Spanish stone house completed in Mérida, in 1549, bears a very graphic celebration of the Conquest.

3 Gran Museo del Mundo Maya

This museum **(below)** has a fascinating array of exhibits from the Mayan world, and an impressive sound and light show on Fridays and weekends.

Map of Mérida

NEED TO KNOW

MAP C2

Visitor Info: Palacio Municipal, Calle 56A, No. 242; (999) 925 5186; www.merida.gob.mx/turismo

Palacio del Gobernador: open 8am–9pm daily

Museo de Antropología: Palacio Cantón; (999) 923 0557; open 8am–5pm Tue–Sun; adm $5; www.inah.gob.mx

Gran Museo del Mundo Maya: Calle 60 Norte, No. 299 E, Unidad Revolución; (999) 341 0435; open 9am–5pm Wed–Mon; adm adults $8; children $1; www.granmuseodel mundomaya.com.mx

■ For some of the best lunches in Mérida, head up to Paseo Montejo away from the main tourist drag. Note that some of the city's upmarket restaurants close in the evenings.

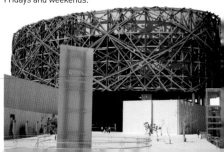

THE TRÍOS

Walk around the Plaza Mayor on most evenings and you'll see groups of men in threes, dressed in white shirts and black trousers, and carrying guitars. These are the Yucatán *tríos*, traditional troubadours available for hire to play romantic serenades. They can be hired to entertain at a party or wedding, or you can have them sing there on the square.

9 Parque Santa Lucía

The arcaded square of Santa Lucía, dating in part from 1575, is the most romantic of all Mérida's old squares. Free concerts of traditional music take place here every Thursday.

10 Iglesia de Jesús

The Jesuits built this church **(below)** in 1618, favoring ornamentation and a little flair over the plain style of the Franciscans, who built most of the city's other religious buildings.

5 Plaza Mayor

This spacious square **(above)** was the heart of the Mayan city of Ti'ho, and so was made into the new city's hub by conquistador Francisco Montejo, when he founded Mérida in 1542. It is still surrounded by the city's main public buildings, while its colonnades and benches set under giant laurel trees provide favorite meeting places.

6 Paseo de Montejo

Laid out in the Yucatán's early 1900s boom in the style of Parisian boulevards, Paseo de Montejo is lined with magnificent mansions, some using Mayan iconography.

7 Market

This is the shopping hub *(see p113)* of the Yucatán, with stalls piled high with food, hammocks, sandals, Panama hats, and embroidery.

8 Museo de Antropología

One of Mexico's most important archaeological museums is set in the grandest of all the Paseo Montejo mansions, built for General Francisco Cantón between 1909 and 1911. It has many treasures excavated from sites across the Yucatán, and is especially rich in ceramics and jade. It offers an overview of the Mayan world that illuminates visits to the site.

🔟 ⭐ Uxmal

The most majestic of the Mayan cities, Uxmal (which means "three-times-built") was a powerful city state from 700 CE to 900 CE. Its spectacular buildings resemble gigantic stage sets and have been compared to the famous monuments of Greece and Rome.

Pyramid of the Magician ❶

Unusually, Uxmal's best-known pyramid **(right)** has rounded corners. The temple at the top is the legendary home of the Dwarf of Uxmal. Sadly, visitors can no longer climb to the top.

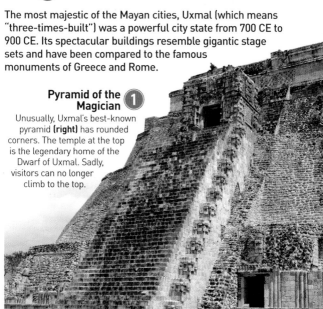

House of the Pigeons ❷

This splendid complex consists of temples and palatial residences, once covered in sculptures. Early travelers thought the lofty roof comb above its central quadrangle looked like dovecotes **(below)**, hence the name.

Temple of the Centipede and the Arch ❸

Unexcavated areas include the Temple of the Centipede. The *sacbé* (Mayan road) leading to it continued to the allied city of Kabah. An arch marks the boundary of Uxmal's central core.

Map of Uxmal

Great Pyramid ❹

Many parts of this towering pyramid are older than the Governor's Palace next door. Like many Mayan buildings, it was altered and added to many times but is now in poor condition.

⑤ House of the Old Woman

Only partly excavated, this large pyramid with a Puuc-style temple on one side is among the oldest major structures at Uxmal, dating from about 700 CE. In Mayan legend, it is said to be the home of the Sprite's Mother.

UXMAL'S SPRITE

In Mayan legend, Uxmal was founded by an *alux* (sprite), who had defied the authority of a local king. When the king dared the sprite to build a house, the Pyramid of the Magician appeared overnight. On another day the sprite built the path to Kabah. The king's last test was that they should both be hit on the head with hammers. The king died, but the sprite was protected by a magic tortilla and went on to rule Uxmal.

⑥ Sound and Light Show

Every night, Uxmal's major buildings are dramatically lit up in varying colors **(above)**, and there is a commentary on Uxmal in history and legend.

⑦ Nunnery Quadrangle

This elegant complex of four buildings was at the heart of Uxmal's power and ritual. It was so named by a Spanish friar merely because its structure reminded him of a convent. Its facade's intricate carvings *(see p36)* symbolize the magical authority of the city and its rulers and their contact with the gods.

⑧ House of the Turtles

This small, delicately proportioned temple-residence is considered the archetype of the pure Puuc architectural style *(see p37)*. The name comes from its decorative cornice, featuring a line of turtles carved in stone. This is a motif that is seen many times at Uxmal; it was associated with the rebirth of new life and the fertility of the coming of the rains.

⑨ Ball Court

Uxmal's main Ball Court is smaller than the Great Court at Chichén Itzá *(see p31)*. The original scoring rings are inscribed with dates from the year 901; those you see at the court are replicas **(above)**.

⑩ Governor's Palace

Often regarded as the finest of all Mayan buildings, this huge palace, over 300 ft (91 m) long, was built for the greatest of Uxmal's rulers, known as Chan-Chak-Kaknal-Ahaw, or Lord Chak. Its huge frieze symbolizes the passage of time as well as the cycles of rain, sun, and rebirth.

Uxmal: The Carvings

1 Monstermouths
Temple entrances in the form of giant monster-like faces, such as on the House of the Dwarf at the Pyramid of the Magician, made a striking connection between the temple and the gods of the earth.

2 Nunnery: Vision Serpents
The patterns on the East Building are Vision Serpents, conduits between men and the "Otherworld."

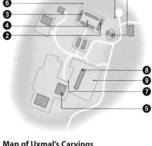

Map of Uxmal's Carvings

Serpent heads at the Nunnery

3 Nunnery: Serpent Heads
The huge feathered snakes winding around the West Building are probably Vision Serpents. Human faces emerge from their jaws.

4 Nunnery Quadrangle: Mayan Huts
A distinctive feature of Puuc carving is the combination of complex symbols with everyday images. The huts carved on the South Building of the Nunnery are very little different from those seen in Yucatecan villages today.

5 Parrots of the Great Pyramid
Stylized *guaca-mayas* (macaws) feature prominently as symbols of uncontrolled nature in the carvings on the temple at the top of the Great Pyramid.

6 Nunnery: Flowers and Lattices
Lattice work represented the huts in which meetings were held, while flowers symbolized magic. The combination of the two denoted a ceremonial site.

7 Muyal Symbols
The simple spiral pattern seen frequently on the Nunnery and Governor's Palace represents the Mayan word for cloud, *muyal*, yet another symbol of contact with the heavens.

8 Lord Chak
The figure in a spectacular headdress set within the facade of the Governor's Palace is believed to be Lord Chak himself.

9 La Picota
The phallic column called the "whipping-post" in Spanish has inscriptions on it that have never been deciphered. It formed part of a fertility cult that was a distinctive feature of Uxmal.

10 Birds Quadrangle
The beautiful images of parrots and other birds carved here symbolized the unpredictable elements in nature.

Parrot carving at the Birds Quadrangle

THE PUUC CITIES

Uxmal was the largest of a string of Mayan communities that flourished in the Puuc Hills of southern Yucatán around 650–920 CE. The other well-known cities are Kabah, Sayil, Xlapak, and Labná *(see pp44–5)*. Their very distinctive style of architecture is the most refined of those used by Mayan builders, and is characterized by strong horizontal lines, elegant proportions, and a sharp contrast between very plain lower walls and rows of elaborately carved friezes above them. Many architectural details seem to mimic humbler buildings and natural features, such as the small drum columns along the bottom of many Puuc walls, which imitate the stick walls of village huts. The communities that lived in these cities were wealthy but fragile, because this region is one of the driest parts of the Yucatán. Indeed, severe drought was probably a major reason why the southern Mayan cities collapsed very quickly, in 800–950 CE *(see p42)*. A one- or two-day tour of the main Puuc cities is possible, following the recognized Puuc Route, south of Uxmal.

TOP 10
PUUC CITIES

1 Oxkintok
2 Uxmal
3 Kabah
4 Sayil
5 Nohpat
6 Xlapak
7 Labná
8 Chacmultún
9 Xcalumkín, Campeche
10 Itzimté, Campeche

Mayan Puuc-style carving can clearly be seen here on the grand Arch of Labná.

Kabah's Codz Poop
The main facade of the Codz Poop (Palace of Masks) at Kabah is covered in over 250 faces of the rain-god Chac *(see p43)*. The Maya believed that covering structures with images of gods gave the buildings divine powers.

🔟 ⭐ Campeche

The Old City of Campeche is a remarkable museum piece of the colonial era. Cobbled streets of aged houses painted in delicate blues, greens, and ochers still sit within the city walls, which were built to fend off pirate attacks when this was one of the great trading strongholds of the Spanish empire. Campeche's actual museum, housed in an old fortress, displays spectacular Mayan relics from the excavated forest city of Calakmul.

1 Palacio Centro Cultural

Housed in an attractive colonial-era building on the Parque Principal, this museum innovatively charts the history of the city through multimedia displays, a sound and light show, and exhibits that include a replica Spanish galleon.

4 Casa Seis

A gracious old house on the west side of the Parque Principal, this has been restored to re-create the home of a prosperous 19th-century Campeche merchant. The house's patio hosts a tourist information desk and also features concerts and exhibitions.

7 Puerta de Tierra

Built in 1732, the Puerta de Tierra ("Land Gate") was the only way in or out of Campeche on the landward side. Within is a museum of maritime and pirate history.

2 Fuerte San Miguel Museum

A hilltop fortress (above) just south of the city, this is now home to a fine collection of Mayan relics, including a set of beautiful jade funeral masks.

5 The Malecón

This waterfront has been attractively restored and is a popular place for locals to take an evening stroll. There are often superb sunsets over the Gulf of Mexico.

3 Museo de las Estelas Mayas

After the city walls were built, Puerta de Mar provided the only gateway to the harbor. The bastion houses the Museo de las Estelas Mayas, displaying Mayan carvings from sites around Campeche.

6 Cathedral

Begun in the 1560s, the cathedral in Campeche (right) was not completed until the 19th century. Its facade is one of the oldest parts, designed in a Spanish Renaissance style typical of many churches built in the reign of King Philip II.

Map of Campeche

Street in Campeche's colonial Old City

Edzná

10 This city (see p112), 30 miles (48 km) south-east of Campeche, once rivalled Chichén Itzá and Uxmal in size and wealth. Its palace-temple, known as the "Building of the Five Stories" (above), is one of the largest, most intricate Mayan buildings.

Baluarte de Santiago

8 This isolated bastion has been imaginatively used to house a dense and verdant botanical garden, with giant palms and other lush tropical flora.

Fuerte San José Museum

9 This sturdy Spanish fortress houses the Post-Conquest sections of the town's museum. There are lovely sea and city views from the ramparts.

NEED TO KNOW

MAP A5

Visitor Info: Casa Seis, Av Ruiz Cortines; (981) 127 3300

Palacio Centro Cultural: Calle 8, between 55–7, Zona Centro; (981) 811 0366, (981) 816 7741; open 10am–7pm Tue–Sun

Museo de las Estelas Mayas: Puerta de Mar; open 8am–5pm Tue–Sun; adm $2

Puerta de Tierra: open 9am–8pm

Fuerte San Miguel Museum: open 8am–5pm Tue–Sun; adm $3.50

Fuerte San José Museum: open 9:30am–5:30pm Tue–Sun; adm $3

■ "El Guapo" trolleys run to the fortress museums from the Parque Principal.

■ Cheerful Luz de Luna (Calle 59, No. 6) offers a range of good-value Mexican dishes.

The Top 10
of Everything

Dancers at the Mérida en Domingo weekly fiesta

Moments in History	**42**	Sports and Activities	**60**
Popular Mayan Sites	**44**	Off the Beaten Path	**62**
Churches	**46**	Children's Attractions	**64**
Spanish-era Towns	**48**	Nightspots	**66**
Beaches	**50**	Dishes of the Yucatán	**68**
Diving Reefs	**52**	Restaurants	**70**
Eco-Parks and Theme Parks	**54**	Cancún and the Yucatán for Free	**72**
Wildlife Reserves	**56**		
Cenotes and Caves	**58**	Festivals	**74**

🔟 Moments in History

① 2000 BCE–100 CE: Early Cultures

The Maya emerged in the Yucatán perhaps as early as 2000 BCE. But it is not until 300 BCE–100 CE that the distinctive characteristics of their culture appeared – such as a writing system, calendar, and city states. For these attributes, the Maya owe much to the first great culture of ancient Mexico, the Olmecs, who thrived between 1500 and 300 BCE.

A rare pre-conquest Mayan codex

② 250–800: Classic Era Mayan Civilization

For over 500 years in the Classic era, Mayan civilization flourished throughout the Yucatán, Chiapas, northern Guatemala, and Belize. And, from about 650, the culture expanded vigorously in the northern Yucatán, reaching its peak at Chichén Itzá and Uxmal.

③ 800–950: Collapse of Mayan Civilization

In the relatively short span of about 150 years, Mayan civilization almost disappeared, most likely due to a series of catastrophes – over-population, over-use of exhausted land, intensification of inter-Mayan wars, and drought. The southern city states were left deserted, and the Mayan writing system virtually disappeared. In the north, the decline occurred later, and the cities were never entirely abandoned.

④ 1150–1520: Post-classic Revival of Mayan Culture

After a 200-year gap, Mayan culture was revived on a modest scale in the northern Yucatán, with the city of Mayapán. Smaller cities, such as Cozumel, El Rey (Cancún), and Tulum developed near the Yucatán coast and became important links in a trade route between the Aztecs of Central Mexico and South America.

⑤ 1517: Spaniards Arrive

An expedition led by Francisco Hernández de Córdoba sailed from Cuba and made the first Spanish landfall in Mexico, on Isla Mujeres. It continued to Campeche and Champotón, but it was then attacked by the Maya and forced to turn back.

⑥ 1526–42: Spanish Invasion of the Yucatán

The Yucatán was invaded and occupied on the third attempt by conquistadores led by three members of the Montejo family. Having been besieged for months in the ruins of ancient Ti'ho, they made it the site of their new city of Mérida.

Painting depicting the conquistadores

Yucatán Independence ceremony

7 1821: Independence

As Spain's American Empire collapsed, the Yucatán, which had had its own administration under Spanish rule, grudgingly agreed to become part of an independent Mexico, but declared independence a few years later. In 1842 a Mexican attempt to reincorporate the Yucatán by force was beaten back.

8 1847: Caste War Begins

Mayans across the Yucatán rose against their white and *mestizo* (mixed-race) rulers in the best-organized Indigenous revolt anywhere in the Americas since the Conquest – and almost succeeded. The main Caste War was over by 1850, but rebels continued to defy Mexico until 1902 – some until 1930.

9 1860–1910: Henequén Boom

Global demand soared for sisal rope, made from the *henequén* agave, transforming the Yucatán's economy. This "green gold" was the world's best rope until the synthetics of the 1950s. New wealth was reflected in Mérida's extravagant mansions, theaters, and other attractions for *henequén* magnates. The boom even partly survived the Mexican Revolution, which began in 1910.

10 1971: Tourism Arrives

Cancún's first hotel opened and another economic transformation began with the dawn of tourism.

TOP 10 GODS AND SPIRITS OF THE ANCIENT MAYA

1 Itzamná
Paramount god in the Post-classic Yucatán, he is the god of medicine and the inventor of writing.

2 Ixchel
The goddess of fertility, childbirth, and weaving.

3 Maize God
One of the foremost gods, created by the First Mother and First Father (maize was essential in ancient America).

4 Hero Twins
In Mayan myths, the twins Hunahpú and Xbalanqué have many adventures and defy the forces of death.

5 Earth Lord
The Maya viewed the earth as a living being, which could be either kindly or monstrous. Monstermouth temples *(see p36)* are often representations of the Earth Lord.

6 Tlaloc
A Central Mexican god of rain and war, with strange "goggles" on his eyes.

7 Kukulcán
A powerful bird-serpent, the Central Mexican god Quetzalcóatl was known in the Yucatán as Kukulcán.

8 Vision Serpents
Conduits between men and the gods, they were summoned up by Mayan lords and shamans during rituals.

9 Cosmic Turtle
Another symbol of water and the earth. In the Mayan creation myth, the Maize God emerges through a crack in the shell of the cosmic turtle.

10 Chac
The Mayan god of rain and lightning, he is identifiable in carvings by his long, curling snout.

Chac, the god of lightning and rain

TOP 10 Popular Mayan Sites

1 Labná
MAP C4

One of the most beautiful Mayan sites, this (see p109) is set in a wooded valley full of colorful birds and retains a strong impression of the life that went on here. It has fine buildings, above all the Arch of Labná.

Doorway in a Labná building

2 Kabah
MAP C4

This (see p110) was second in importance among the Puuc cities (see p37) after Uxmal, to which it was linked by a *sacbé* or Mayan road. A grand arch over the end of this path forms a pair with the arch at Uxmal (see pp34–7). The great highlight is the Codz-Poop or "Palace of Masks," with a facade that has over 250 long-nosed Chac faces.

Buildings in the Kabah complex

3 Ek-Balam
MAP F2

This compact city (see p102) was little known, but excavations of its largest temple-mound in 1998 revealed spectacular carvings, especially at El Trono ("The Throne"), the largest and most extravagant of Mayan monster-mouth temples. Other unique buildings include an almost spiral-shaped tower, La Redonda, the design of which is a mystery.

4 Sayil
MAP C4

With around 17,000 inhabitants in 850 CE, Sayil (see p110) was among the wealthiest of the Puuc towns. Its magnificent Palacio has been likened to ancient Greek buildings. The Mirador pyramid was the center of the town's market area.

5 Dzibilchaltún
MAP C2

Located just north of Mérida, this site (see p110) was occupied for over 2,000 years. At dawn on spring and summer equinoxes, the sun strikes straight through the open doorways of the Temple of the Seven Dolls and along a road. There's also a great swimming cenote located here.

6 Chichén Itzá
MAP E3

The most dramatic of the Mayan cities, this (see pp28–31) has gigantic buildings, including the great pyramid that has become an enduring symbol of the Yucatán.

Tulum
MAP G4

A small city from the last decades of Mayan civilization, Tulum (see pp22–3) is spectacular as the only Mayan city built above a beach.

8 Edzná
MAP B5

One of the largest and wealthiest cities of Classic-era Yucatán (see p42), Edzná (see p39) features a huge palace, the "Building of the Five Stories," which is the largest and most complex of all Mayan multistory buildings.

9 Uxmal
MAP C4

A hugely atmospheric city, Uxmal (see pp34–7) has some of the finest Mayan buildings in the Nunnery Quadrangle and the Governor's Palace.

Pyramid of the Magician, Uxmal

10 Cobá
MAP F3

Before the rise of Chichén Itzá, Cobá (see p92) was the largest and most powerful city in northern Yucatán. Buildings are spread over a huge area of dense forest and lakes. The Nohoch Mul, at 138 ft (42 m), is the highest pyramid in the Yucatán.

TOP 10 QUIETER SITES

Aké's strange stone columns

1 Aké
MAP C2
Built of massive columns and huge stone slabs, this city (see 101) is unlike anywhere else in the Yucatán.

2 El Meco, Cancún
The most important place (see p82) near Cancún in pre-Hispanic times.

3 San Gervasio, Cozumel
Capital of the island when it (see pp14–15) was one of the great pilgrimage centers of Mayan Yucatán.

4 Xel-Ha
One (see p23) of the oldest Mayan sites near the modern Riviera, with ancient murals of birds.

5 Muyil
A very old Mayan site (see p26) next to the Sian Ka'an reserve, with several pyramids amid the forest.

6 El Rey, Cancún
The relics (see p13) of the historic occupiers of Cancún Island.

7 Xcambó
MAP C2
A tiny site (see p104) with a Catholic chapel built onto one of its pyramids.

8 Oxkintok
MAP B3
Ancient city (see p112) just west of the Puuc area. It rivalled Uxmal in size, and it has a bizarre temple-labyrinth.

9 Xlapak
MAP C4
The Palacio has a frieze of elaborately carved Chac-masks (see p112).

10 Mayapán
MAP C3
The last major Mayan city (see p112), which dominated the Yucatán from 1200–1400.

🔟 Churches

① San Antonio de Padua, Izamal
MAP D2

The monastery of Izamal *(see p48)*, painted ocher and white like the rest of the town, epitomizes the plain, austere style favored by the Franciscan friars, who brought Catholicism to the Yucatán. It was founded in 1549, and its huge *atrio*, or courtyard, was designed to hold great crowds of Mayans worshipping in open-air Masses.

② San Bernardino Sisal, Valladolid
MAP E3

The oldest permanent church in the Yucatán began as part of a Franciscan monastery in 1552. It was located outside Valladolid *(see p102)* in order to function both as a place of worship for the Spanish townsfolk and as a mission for Mayan villagers. Inside is a spectacularly painted Baroque altarpiece. The cloister surrounds an overgrown, palm-filled garden with a massive stone well from 1613, built over a cenote.

San Bernardino Sisal, Valladolid

Retable carving, Maní Monastery

③ Maní Monastery
MAP C4

The first of all the Franciscan missionary monasteries in the Yucatán, consecrated in 1549, Maní *(see p49)* was built very simply, with a massive stone facade and cavernous cloister. Set within the facade was an external altar or "Indian Chapel," so that open-air services could be held in the square. In 1562, after the Franciscans discovered that many Mayans were practising their old religion in secret, an *auto da fé* was held in the square, during which the friars burned hundreds of Mayan manuscripts and pagan relics.

④ La Mejorada, Mérida
MAP C2

This large church with a very Spanish-looking plain facade was built as part of a major Franciscan friary in 1640. It was the last occupied monastery in Mérida, and closed only in 1857. Behind the church, some of the former monastery buildings now house a school of architecture.

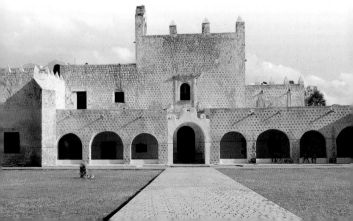

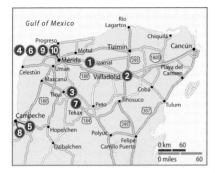

added only in the 1750s, and that on its right as late as the 1850s.

9 Iglesia de Jesús, Mérida
MAP C2

Built for the Jesuit Order and completed in 1618, the Jesús (see p33) has a gilded Baroque interior that contrasts strikingly with the simplicity of the Franciscan churches. On the exterior, look out for traces of carvings on some of the stones – these were taken from Mayan temples.

5 San Roque, Campeche
MAP A5

Campeche's churches are generally more colorful than those of Mérida and central Yucatán. San Roque is an extravagant example of Mexican Baroque, with a beautifully restored opulent altarpiece that is surrounded by intricate white plasterwork.

6 Las Monjas, Mérida
MAP C2

The church of "The Nuns" was built in the 1590s as a chapel for one of the first closed convents in the Americas. The castle-like mirador, or watchtower, with its unusual loggia (covered balcony) was built so that the nuns could take the air without leaving the convent. Somber metal grills inside the church recall the separation that was kept between nuns and lay worshippers.

7 Tekax Church
MAP C4

Completed in 1692, this huge yet finely proportioned church was built in a lighter style than those of the early colonial period. The churches at Teabo (see p48) and Oxkutzcab (see p49) are similar.

8 Campeche Cathedral
MAP A5

Mérida and Campeche began their cathedrals around the same time, but the stop-start construction at Campeche meant that while the central facade was finished during the 1600s, the tower on its left was

Around Mérida Cathedral

10 Mérida Cathedral
MAP C2

The first cathedral (see p32) built in mainland America was constructed by local conquistadores in a style that the church leaders found extravagant. The design is, in fact, simple, with few flourishes, and the solemn interior is set in white stone. The figures that you pass on the way in represent saints Peter and Paul.

🔟 Spanish-era Towns

Valladolid cathedral and main square

1 Valladolid

The city is a combination of distinguished colonial architecture and the easygoing atmosphere of a Yucatán market town. Whitewashed arcades and 17th-century houses surround the main plaza, and among the town's many old Spanish houses and churches is a fine Franciscan monastery *(see p46)*. Just off the plaza, Casa de los Venados houses one of Mexico's finest collections of modern folk art. Four blocks away is the dramatic pit of Cenote Zací, once Valladolid's main source of water.

2 Tizimín

The city's name comes from the Mayan *tsimin*, a kind of demon, also used to describe the Spaniards when they first appeared on horse-back. Today the town *(see p104)* is the capital of Yucatán's "cattle country," between Valladolid and Río Lagartos. Its pleasant twin central plazas are divided by two huge monasteries, giving it a distinctly Mediterranean appearance.

3 Teabo
MAP C4

With an air of pleasant tranquility, this remote town clusters around its grand and lofty Franciscan church, built in 1650–95. In the sacristy are rare murals of saints, discovered by accident in the 1980s. Teabo is also known for its fine embroidery.

4 Izamal

Known as La Ciudad Dorada, the Golden City *(see p103)*, because of the ocher wash of its buildings, this is the most complete and unchanged of Yucatán colonial towns. At its heart is the largest of the Yucatán's Franciscan monasteries *(see p46)*, and a short distance from this are the pyramids of a much older Mayan city.

The yellow colonial city of Izamal

Ancient Mayan pyramid, Acanceh

8 Mérida

The capital *(see pp32–3)* of the Yucatán, which was founded by the Spaniards in 1542 on the site of the ancient Mayan city of Ti'ho, is truly charming. Whitewashed Spanish houses with shaded patios provide delightful places to stay. Despite the bustle of its market (and traffic), amid the city's old squares daily life still proceeds at a leisurely, friendly pace.

9 Campeche

The most complete Spanish walled city in Mexico, Campeche *(see pp38–9)* is full of reminders of the era when it was a trading hub of Spain's empire and looked upon with greed by Caribbean pirates. The old city – complete with its churches, patios, Andalusian-style grill windows, and facades in delicate pastel colors – has been restored to refresh its distinctive Hispanic character and charm.

5 Acanceh
MAP C3

An extraordinary little town in which over 2,000 years of time are on show, from its ancient Mayan edifices to a fine 18th-century Spanish church.

6 Ticul

With a friendly atmosphere, Ticul is the epitome of a small Yucatán country town and makes an excellent base for visiting Puuc *(see p37)*. Shoes are the town's traditional product, and it also has a museum dedicated to chocolate, featuring live demonstrations and cultural re-enactments.

7 Oxkutzcab
MAP C4

The south of Yucatán near the Puuc hills is a fertile, fruit-producing region. Oxkutzcab has a huge market, where Mayan women in *huípiles* (white blouses with bright embroidery) preside over stalls stacked with succulent mangoes, papaya, oranges, watermelons, and more. Above them stands the lofty tower of the town church, finished in 1645.

10 Maní
MAP C4

Now wonderfully tranquil, Mani was important at the time of the Spanish invasion, and contains the oldest Franciscan missionary *(see p46)* monastery in the Yucatán, the scene of dramatic events in 1562. The town was the seat of Tutul Xiu, the first of the Mayan lords to accept Spanish authority in 1542. The monastery and town square are situated on the top of an old Mayan temple-platform.

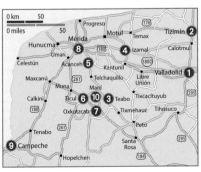

🔟 Beaches

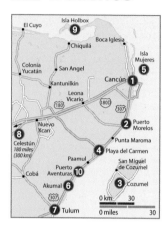

③ Cozumel
The island's (see pp14–15) fan base is split into three: divers, cruise passengers, and families. The finest diving locations are in the distant reefs, but the tranquil beaches along Cozumel's west coast are wonderful for a first experience of snorkeling. San Miguel town has a touristy but easygoing feel.

Beachgoers at Playa del Carmen

① Cancún
This resort (see pp12–13) has the longest stretch of beach, backed by the biggest hotels and malls, and with the most attractions, ranging from parasailing to water parks. The beaches on the north side of the island are the best for swimming and beach-life, but they can get rather crowded. On the surf beaches along the east it is always possible to find a spot to yourself, but check safety conditions.

④ Playa del Carmen
This popular spot (see pp16–17) on the Mayan Riviera offers good shopping, strolling, bar-hanging, and people-watching opportunities. It also has miles of lovely palm-lined bays stretching away to the north. To the south, the Playacar development has its own narrower beaches.

Azure waters off Puerto Morelos

② Puerto Morelos
Despite its location between Cancún and Playa del Carmen, Puerto Morelos (see p79) has avoided big-scale development. There's plenty of space along the long, white beach, where pelicans hang in the wind. A great snorkeling reef (see p52) lies close to the shore.

⑤ Isla Mujeres
Isla's small size (see pp20–21) means it has a more laid-back beach scene, especially on Playa Norte by Isla town, with its placid, safe waters. The island is a good-value diving center.

⑥ Akumal
This is a lovely area (see p92) that extends through beautiful, sweeping bays of white sands and

gentle seas. Some big hotels have opened, but secluded and low-key condominium apartments and villas can be found located along most of the bays. Akumal *(see p52)* is also an excellent diving center.

7 Tulum

The most favored place *(see pp22–3)* in the Yucatán for anyone wanting to settle into a palm-roofed cabin by a beach for a while *(see p52)*. Head to the north end for cheap cabins where you will get to know your neighbors, or turn south for more secluded and comfortable cabins.

8 Celestún

Most tourists go to Celestún *(see p57)* only to see its flamingos, but it is also a tranquil village *(see p109)* with an endless white-sand beach lined by fishing boats. There are some very enjoyable beach restaurants *(see p115)* and often wonderful sunsets over the Gulf of Mexico.

9 Isla Holbox

One of the hippest destinations in the Yucatán, particularly amongst backpackers, Isla Holbox has attractive beaches facing onto the Gulf of Mexico. From May to mid-September the waters are home to endangered whale sharks, which can be spotted on boat and snorkelling trips.

Sailing off Puerto Aventuras

10 Puerto Aventuras

This Mediterranean-style resort town was purpose-built from scratch around a natural inlet in the coast. It now contains the Riviera's best-equipped yachting marina, surrounded by a smart holiday village of villas and condo apartments. A variety of aquatic activities are offered here. There's also a golf course, tennis center, and several large hotels.

White-sand beach at Isla Holbox

🔟 Diving Reefs

Manchones reef, Isla Mujeres

of experience, and visibility is ideal. Paraíso and nearby Chankanaab are "must-sees," with strangely shaped coral just below the surface.

① Manchones, Isla Mujeres
MAP L2

A fascinatingly varied reef, half a mile (1 km) long, but only 30 ft (9 m) deep for much of it. The Sac Bajo area, just off the lagoon south of Isla Town, is excellent for snorkeling, and there are spectacular reefs farther from the island (see pp20–21).

② Tankah
MAP P6

This less well-known beach (see p94) with just a few hotels is great for relaxed snorkeling and diving away from the crowds. As at Akumal, the reef is quite close to the shore.

③ Paraíso, Cozumel
MAP R5

Cozumel (see pp14–15) offers the greatest extent and variety of reef for snorkelers and divers of every level

④ Puerto Morelos
MAP R3

One of the most vibrant of the mainland beaches and officially protected as a *parque maritimo*. The reef is unusually close to the shore, so it is great for snorkel tours and introductory diving. The few dive and snorkel operators here offer a personal, friendly service.

⑤ Akumal
MAP P5

The beaches here (see p92) provide an important breeding area for sea turtles, which coexist with the development along the bays. The reefs fringing the beaches are wonderful for snorkeling and diving. Akumal is also an important cave-diving center, with Aquatech based at the Villas de Rosa Beach Resort (see p130).

⑥ Tulum
MAP P6

This (see pp22–3) is the Riviera's biggest center for cave-diving (see pp58–9), but dive operators also take snorkelers and divers to the reefs nearby, in a deliciously clear sea.

Cave-diving at Tulum

Reefs around Cancún
MAP K4 & K6

Despite busy beaches and the relatively small size of the closest reefs, there's still lots to see here (see pp12–13). "Jungle" snorkeling tours take you through mangroves in Laguna Nichupté and to the reef off Punta Nizuc.

8 Playa del Carmen and Chunzubul
MAP Q4

Several high-standard dive operators are based in Playa (see pp16–17), taking divers to the reefs nearby and elsewhere along the Riviera.

Corals of Palancar, Cozumel

Palancar, Cozumel
MAP Q6

An extraordinary coral mountain (see pp14–15) with giant canyons that plunge straight from the surface to the depths of the ocean. Nearby, the Yucab and El Cedral reefs are famous for colonies of moray eels and groupers, and tree-like coral heads.

Xpu-Ha
MAP P5

The superb reefs offshore here (see p93) are a favorite destination for Playa del Carmen dive operators. Angelfish, triggerfish, and parrotfish are abundant, along with a luxuriant range of coral.

TOP 10 REEF ANIMALS

1 Fan Corals
Delicately veined fronds coming up from the ocean floor and wave graciously in the undersea currents.

2 Sea Cucumbers
Tube-like creatures with a tough, spiny skin that can be seen lying motionless on the seabed or in clefts in the coral.

3 Snappers
Among the commonest fish here, yellowtail, blackfin, and other snappers move in huge, gleaming shoals.

4 Angelfish
Spectacularly colorful fish, with a fan-like shape and luminous stripes and patches in vibrant yellows and electric blue.

5 Sergeant Majors
Bright, darting little fish, easily recognizable by their black and yellow vertical stripes.

6 Pufferfish
Bizarre fish that, when provoked, inflate themselves by taking in water in order to deter attackers.

7 Parrotfish
These come in many varieties and sizes, but most are very colorful and look as if they are smiling amiably.

8 Rays
Spotted eagle rays, elegantly waving their "wings", are common around some of the Cozumel reefs.

9 Barracudas and Sharks
Many varieties are found around the Yucatán reefs – but attacks on humans are almost unknown.

10 Turtles
Now endangered, sea turtles come ashore to lay their eggs on sandy beaches along the southern Riviera.

An endangered sea turtle

ᴛᴏᴘ10 Eco-Parks and Theme Parks

① Laguna Chankanaab, Cozumel

This small nature and snorkeling park *(see p14)* lies close to the Chankanaab and Paraíso reefs *(see p52)* and includes a beach, a botanical garden, and a spa. Activities such as scuba diving and snorkeling are also available.

② Aqua World, Cancún

MAP K5 ▪ Blvd Kukulcán, km 15.2 ▪ (998) 848 8326 ▪ Open 7am–8pm daily ▪ Charges per activity ▪ www.aquaworld.com.mx

A multiactivity fun center on Cancún Island, Aqua World offers jungle tours, submarine rides, jetskiing, snorkeling, diving, fishing, parasailing, dinner cruises, and tours to Isla Mujeres and Cozumel.

Scuba diving at Aqua World

③ Ventura Park

The biggest water park *(see p64)* in town has a 350-yd (320-m) lazy river and a kids' park. But the best highlight of all is the actual water park *(see p82)*, with slides, rides, and wave pools for all ages, making this the perfect spot for the whole family.

Parque Garrafón on Isla Mujeres

④ Parque Garrafón, Isla Mujeres

MAP L2 ▪ (1) 866 393 5158 ▪ Open 8:30am–6:30pm (winter: until 5pm) ▪ Adm ▪ www.garrafon.com

A broad, natural pool of rock and coral is the central attraction. There's also a swimming pool, and snorkeling reefs just offshore. The calm waters make it good for novices, while hiking and biking trails offer a change of scene.

⑤ Dos Ojos Cenote

The upper chambers of the world's longest underwater cave system, the Dos Ojos Cenote *(see p94)*, are used by the diving tours for one of the Yucatán's most exciting tours. Visitors can snorkel or scuba dive through crystal-clear cave waters in giant arched-roof caverns *(see p23)*.

⑥ Xplor

Located 4 miles (6 km) south of Playa del Carmen, Xplor *(see pp80–81)* is the Riviera Maya's biggest adventure park. Fourteen ziplines, including Cancún's longest, take visitors soaring above the jungle canopy to splashdown landings in cool, cenote waters. Visitors can drive amphibious vehicles across rope bridges and through grottoes and jungle, paddle a raft on warm, clear waters through subterranean caverns, and swim along underground rivers amid stalactites and stalagmites.

7 Aktun-Chen

MAP P5 ■ (984) 806 4962
■ **Open 9:30am–5:30pm daily** ■ **Adm (prices vary by activity)** ■ www. aktun-chenpark.com

From the highway near Akumal, a dirt track leads west through thick bromeliad-filled jungle to a nature park set around a vast cave and cenote system. Swim and zipline across the cenote and take guided tours through the stalactite-filled cavern, which is highly impressive. Colorful birds, monkeys, and wild boars can be seen outside.

8 Xel-Ha

One of the Riviera's most popular attractions, this snorkel park (see p65) was created around a magnificent natural coastal lagoon (see p92). The park is especially good for children and has a special area called the Children's World where the little ones can have their own adventures. It may seem crowded at first, but if you swim a bit away from the landing stages, you'll still find plenty of fish and coral to admire in peace and quiet. There are also some lovely forest trails to explore.

9 Xplor Fuego

MAP Q4 ■ **Carretera Chetumal, Puerto Juarez km 282** ■ **Open 5:30–11:30pm Mon–Sat** ■ **Adm (advance online booking)** ■ www.xcaret.com

This Playa del Carmen-based park operates at night only. It offers jungle rides on amphibious vehicles, ziplining under the stars, and swimming or boating through stalactite-studded caves. An all-you-can-eat buffet is available from 6:30pm onwards.

10 Xcaret

The Riviera's original eco-park (see pp18–19) provides a spectacular introduction to the richness and variety of a tropical environment.

Lush natural setting of Xcaret

🔟 Wildlife Reserves

Beautiful lagoons of Isla Contoy

1 Isla Contoy
MAP H1

This uninhabited island (see p21) reserve north of Isla Mujeres is home to a huge range of sea birds, including pelicans, boobies, and frigate birds, and contains mangroves, turtle-breeding beaches, and superb coral lagoons. One-day tours are run by many dive shops and agencies from Isla and Cancún; check what is included in your tour.

2 Campeche Petenes
MAP A4 ■ Boats for hire in the village of Isla Arena, and tours are offered in Campeche

The north of Campeche State behind the coast consists of *petenes*, which are "islands" of solid land

within the swamp that have special microclimates all of their own, and mangrove lagoons. Within the area are flamingos, deer, and even pumas. Visitor facilities are very limited.

3 Puerto Morelos
MAP R3

The reef off Puerto Morelos (see p52) is one of the least disturbed sections of coral near the mainland in the northern part of the Maya reef and is now protected as a marine park. Snorkelers can see spectacular marine life – lobsters, giant sponges, luminous parrot fish, and angelfish. Dive operators in the town offer low-impact snorkel and diving tours.

4 Sian Ka'an Biosphere Reserve
MAP F6

Biggest by far of the Yucatán's nature reserves, this vast expanse (see pp26–7) of empty forest, mangroves, and lagoons gives an extraordinary glimpse of nature almost untouched by human habitation, and in all its complexity. Tulum is the starting point for organized trips into the reserve.

Boat-billed heron, Sian Ka'an

5 Punta Laguna
MAP N4 ■ Open daily

Spider monkeys are quite common in the Yucatán but often hard to see. Set in very dense forest around a lake near Cobá, this village-run reserve (see p94) is one of the places to find them. Villagers will guide you to the best spots, and monkeys are most likely to be around in the early morning and early afternoon.

A flock of flamingos taking off from a creek at Río Lagartos

6 Río Lagartos
MAP F1

A huge, long, narrow lagoon of creeks, mangroves, and mud and salt flats runs along the north coast of Yucatán and it is tinged pink with colonies of 20,000 flamingos in the peak August breeding season. Fascinating, great-value boat trips are run from Río Lagartos (see p102) and nearby San Felipe (see p63).

7 Bocas de Dzilam
MAP D1 ■ Boatmen in Río Lagartos, San Felipe, and Dzilam Bravo can be hired to take you to the mangrove lagoons ■ Trips last a full day

Much more remote, this giant expanse of uninhabited mangrove lagoons extends west of San Felipe and also contains flamingo colonies and a variety of birds and other undisturbed wildlife. Getting there, with a boat trip over open sea, is a real adventure.

8 Celestún
MAP A3

The most famous flamingo colonies in the Yucatán are in the lagoon (see p109) beside this little town (see p63) on the west coast. Launches run from a visitor center toward the pink streaks of flamingos on the horizon, passing fishers' huts and ibises and many other birds – an ornithologist's delight.

9 Punta Sur Eco Beach Park, Cozumel
MAP R6

This large area (see p15) across the southern tip of Cozumel has an impressive variety of landscapes – forest, dunes, turtle beaches, reefs, and tranquil mangrove lagoons – plus crocodiles, flamingos, and countless other birds. There are observation towers, an information center, and a maritime museum, and you can climb the Punta Celaraín lighthouse.

Crocodile, Punta Sur Eco Park, Cozumel

10 Uaymitún
MAP C2 ■ Donations welcomed

For easy bird-watching in the lagoons along the northern Yucatán coast, this free viewing tower by the coast road east of Progreso is a good option; it even provides binoculars. The top offers spectacular views over the wetlands to the south, and you can see flamingos, ducks, egrets, and, in winter, countless migratory birds from North America.

🔟 Cenotes and Caves

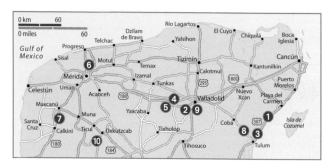

1️⃣ Cenote and Eco-Park Kantun-Chi
MAP P5

There are several cenotes on the landward side of the highway near Xpu-Ha that can be easily accessed by visitors. A broad, shady pool dappled by brilliant sunlight, Kantun-Chi *(see p82)* is near the road but refreshing for swimming. The neighboring cenotes of Cristalino and Azul are also beautiful.

Cavern-pool of Cenote Samula

2️⃣ Cenote Samula

Past a narrow entrance there's a huge pool of cool, clear water *(see p101)* and, in the cave, the roots of a giant ceiba tree – associated with mystical powers by the Maya – stretch straight down from the surface to reach the water far below. Visitors can place their belongings in lockers and take a dip in the water.

3️⃣ Dos Ojos Cenote
MAP P6

This cavern *(see p54)* is called "Two Eyes" because its two entrances look like eyes when seen from above. Extending over 350 miles (563 km) through a labyrinth of caverns and limestone "trees," it has been considered the world's longest underwater cave system – but the nearby Nohoch Nah Chich cenote may be even longer. Inexperienced divers get most from it with the diving tours.

4️⃣ Balankanché Caves
MAP E3 ▪ Open daily, guided tours only ▪ Adm

Alongside several cenote pools and underwater rivers, the Yucatán is underlain by a massive web of dry caves that were sacred places to the ancient Maya. Balankanché *(see p100)*, near Chichén Itzá, is one of the largest and most extraordinary cave systems of all.

5️⃣ Sacred Cenote, Chichén Itzá
MAP E3 ▪ Adm as for Chichén Itzá

The most celebrated cenote in the Yucatán, the giant sacred well at Chichén *(see p29)* has long been said to have been a place of human sacrifice. The cenote was used only for ritual purposes, perhaps as a channel to the Underworld, since the city's drinking water came from the Xtoloc Cenote, near the Caracol.

6 Cenote Xlacah, Dzibilchaltún

The wide cenote that provided water for the ancient city of Dzibilchaltún *(see p110)* is still a popular swimming hole today. It gets busy on Sundays but is great for a dip at other times.

7 Calcehtok
MAP B3

These caves near the Mayan site at Oxkintok *(see p112)* are little-known but are some of the region's most extraordinary. The roofless main chamber is big enough to contain whole trees, and is full of birds.

8 Gran Cenote
MAP N6 ■ Open 8am–5pm daily ■ Adm

The loveliest of the several cenotes along the road from Tulum to Cobá, Gran Cenote is home to a placid, clear pool. Snorkelers and divers can make their way through a massive arched cavern and down a tunnel.

9 Cenote Dzitnup

The most famous of the swimmable cenotes in the region, this awe-inspiring limestone cathedral *(see p101)* has a perfect turquoise pool. It is entered through a narrow tunnel. Tours visit at about 11am, but at other times it's rarely crowded.

Dramatic Loltún Caves

10 Loltún Caves

An astonishing cave system, Loltún Caves *(see p111)* is not far from the Puuc cities *(see p37)*. These caves have the longest history of human habitation in the Yucatán. Chambers are full of bizarre and interesting rock formations, strange airflows, and relics of their Mayan occupants.

Cenote Dzitnup's perfect pool

🔟 Sports and Activities

Spectacular bird's-eye view of a golf course in Cancún's Hotel Zone

1 Golf
Club de Golf Cancún: (987) 267 9653 ▪ Puerto Aventuras Golf Club: (984) 873 5109 ▪ Palace Resort: (01) 800 635 1836; www.palaceresorts.com
Golfers on the Riviera have a choice of two championship-level courses at Cancún, one in Playacar and one at Puerto Aventuras. Hotels can book greens for you. North of Mérida there is also a private club, which is also booked through hotels.

2 Sailing, Windsurfing, and Kayaking
Aqua World: (998) 689 1013; www.aquaworld.com.mx
The best places to rent boats are Isla Mujeres and Cozumel. Hotels may

Kayaking on the Riva Maya

have dinghies available for use by guests. A day's sailing is a great way to explore lesser-known stretches of the coast. Windsurfing is at its finest around Isla Mujeres and Akumal, and the best spots for kayaking are around Puerto Morelos and Punta Solimán (see p95).

3 Diving
Scuba Cancun: (998) 849 7508; www.scubacancun.com.mx
The Mayan Riviera is the site of the second-largest reef in the world. Scuba Cancun offers diving opportunities in Cancún, Riviera Maya, and Cozumel.

4 Fishing
Conditions for deep-sea and inshore fishing in the Yucatán are outstanding, and the lagoons south of the Riviera by Ascencion Bay are a must for fly-fishing fans. The peak deep-sea fishing season runs from March to June.

5 Tennis
RIU Caribe Hotel: (998) 848 7850 ▪ Hotel Omni: (998) 848 7850
Many resort hotels have tennis courts. In Cancún, Hotel Omni's courts are open to all, while those at RIU Caribe Hotel are for residents only. The Club de Golf Cancún also has two courts.

6 Cycling

The most attractive towns for cycling are Cancún, Isla Mujeres, Tulum, and Valladolid, which has a lovely cycle path to Cenote Dzitnup (see p59). Many Cancún hotels have bikes, and there are rental shops in the other three destinations.

7 Skydiving

Sky Dive Playa: (984) 873 0192; www.skydive.com.mx
Sky Dive Playa will offer visitors a bird's-eye view of the Riviera as they plummet down harnessed to an instructor, or on their own if they have skydiving experience.

8 Air Tours

Aerosaab: (998) 865 4225; www.aerosaab.com ■ Fly Tours Cancun: flytourscancun.com
Aerosaab at Playa del Carmen and Fly Tours Cancún at Cancún offer aerial sightseeing tours over the Riviera, Chichén Itzá, and other parts of the Yucatán Peninsula.

Parasailing over Cancún

9 Parasailing

Soar above Cancún with the "Skyrider" at Aqua World. More basic operations are to be found at Cancún beach and at Playa del Carmen.

10 Jungle Tours

Alltournative: 1 877 432 1569, www.alltournative.com ■ ATV Explorer: (984) 873 1626; www.playadelcarmen tours.com/atv-explorer.htm
Playa-based ATV Explorer lets you race through the jungle on four-wheel ATVs. Alltournative runs group trips by truck, jeep, and kayak.

TOP 10 FISHING LOCATIONS

Fishing boats in Puerto Morelos

1 Puerto Morelos
Much lower key than the islands, but deep water close to shore means superb fishing.

2 Isla Mujeres
Highly regarded by deep-sea fishing enthusiasts, with able captains who seek out amberjack, marlin, and more.

3 Cozumel
A base for many expert deep-sea captains, who also offer trips to the inshore flats.

4 Cancún
For easy-access, fun fishing, with trips available from watersports centers such as Aqua World (see p54).

5 Playa del Carmen
Many Playa dive shops also arrange fishing trips, especially in the sailfishing season (March–June).

6 Puerto Aventuras
The most luxuriously equipped fishing center on the coast. Hosts a big deep-sea tournament each May.

7 Boca Paila and Punta Allen
Fly-fishing and, above all, bonefish followers make their way to the remote fishing lodges along this road.

8 Isla Holbox
A long way from the conveniences of the Riviera, but loved by fishers who like a really relaxing time.

9 El Cuyo
The one bar, La Conchita, is the place to go to find a boat and a guide. Shark fishing is a specialty of the north coast.

10 Río Lagartos
No well-organized facilities here, but boatmen will show you their fishing grounds as well as the flamingo lagoons.

🔟 Off the Beaten Path

Punta Allen's peaceful beach

1 Punta Allen
MAP G5

The atrocious state of the road keeps visitor numbers down, but the trek deep into Sian Ka'an (four-wheel-drive only) takes you to a tiny fishing village *(see p26)* of sand streets and giant palms, with landing stages by the beach and a few easy-going restaurants and welcoming places to stay. Local guides offer snorkeling, bird-watching, and fishing trips.

2 Río Lagartos and San Felipe
MAP E–F1

Celebrated for the spectacular flocks of flamingos *(see p57)* in the lagoon to their east, these villages delight visitors with their unhurried, easy-going style. There are great seafood restaurants too, as well as some pleasant small hotels, and, from San Felipe *(see pp102–3)*, wonderful sunsets.

3 Puerto Morelos
MAP R3

An undisturbed gem of the Mexican Caribbean, Puerto Morelos *(see p56)* has kept its mellow, fishing-village *(see p79)* feel despite its close proximity to Cancún. There is no real nightlife to be found here, but there are lovely beaches, and many small apartments and hotels here offer long-term rates.

4 Punta Bete
MAP R4

A well-rutted track off the main highway just north of Playa del Carmen leads in 2 bumpy miles (3 km) to superb, curving beaches of dazzling white sand and a perfect turquoise sea. Some resort hotels have opened up here *(see p79)*, but there are still clusters of laid-back beach *cabañas (see p129)* tucked away among the palms.

Tranquil lagoon of Río Lagartos and San Felipe

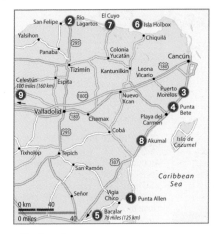

occupied only by a few small-scale hotels and condo apartments. It's quite easy to find uncrowded space at Akumal (see p88), by an idyllic sea and with creature comforts included. There are also some excellent diving facilities here.

9 Celestún
MAP A2

Flamingos, again, are the big attraction here (see p57) but, if you stay over in one of the small hotels after the day-trippers have returned to Mérida, you will be able to make the most of a delightfully peaceful little village (see p109), its beach strewn with fishing boats. North of Celestún is a really remote beach retreat (see p129) at Xixim.

5 Bacalar

Several hours south of Tulum, just north of Mexico's border with Belize, is Bacalar, one of Mexico's Pueblos Mágicos, or Magical Towns. Often referred to as the "Maldives of Mexico," this spot is known for its "Seven Color Lagoon," an enchanting place where seven colors of blue-green can be seen in the water.

6 Isla Holbox
MAP G1

If the Riviera seems too busy, take a long drive north to the tiny port of Chiquilá. Hop on a ferry to cross the beautiful lagoon (where dolphins are common) to reach the island of Holbox (see p51). Here you'll find (see p83) the simple pleasures of a friendly village, a long, empty beach, and some mellow places to stay.

7 El Cuyo
MAP F1

With just one hotel, two sets of beach cabañas, and a couple of places to eat – with great fresh fish – this Gulf coast fishing village (see p104) is for anyone who really does want a beach all to themselves.

8 Akumal
MAP P5

Not a remote spot, but the curving beaches here are very long and often

Pool at the Hacienda Temozon

10 Hacienda Hotels

An enticing escape is offered (at upscale prices) by the hotels scattered around the Yucatán in beautifully converted old colonial haciendas (see pp127–8), which are country estates. All have luxurious rooms surrounded by tropical gardens, with superb pools and fine restaurants.

🔟 Children's Attractions

① Ventura Park, Cancún

Known as the number one fun center *(see p54)* in the region, this water park has much to offer. In addition to the adrenaline-pumping rides that older kids love – the Wave Pool, Bubba Tub, Kamikaze, Double Space Bowl, and Twister, Ventura Park *(see p82)* also has a Kids' Park with rides and slides for young children, so that even the littlest members of the family can join in the fun.

Families snorkeling at Xcaret

② Xcaret

The first and most famous of the eco-parks, Xcaret *(see pp18–19)* provides lots for kids to enjoy, in an easy, family-centered environment. The snorkeling river is a big hit, but children can also enjoy the zoo, butterfly garden, and forest paths. A part of the park has been created especially for children and has, amongst other things, water slides, hanging bridges, and tunnels.

③ Río Secreto

MAP Q4 ▪ (984) 877 2377
▪ www.riosecreto.com

This amazing underground cave and river system is located just south of Playa del Carmen. Don a wet suit and helmet to explore the river that flows 82 ft (25 m) below the surface and see the many spectacular stalagmites and stalactites.

④ Xcacel Beach

Seven of the world's eight marine turtle species nest on the shores of the Yucatán, including green sea and loggerhead turtles. The turtles, many of which are endangered, are vigorously protected by Mexican authorities, and many of the Yucatán's nesting areas have been turned into reserves and sanctuaries. At several of these spots, visitors can help biologists and other officials during nesting season, including at Xcacel Beach *(see p82)*, just 40 minutes south of Playa del Carmen.

⑤ Uxmal

MAP C4

A Mayan site that is well-liked by kids is Uxmal *(see pp34–7)*. Not only does it have lots of steps and temples for running and exploring, but it is also home to many iguanas, which sit stock still until surprised, then dart off with sudden alacrity. Some are as big as crocodiles, but they're all harmless.

6 Xel-Ha
MAP P6 ■ (998) 251 6560
■ Open 8:30am–6pm daily ■ Adm
■ www.xelha.com

This snorkel park *(see p92)* is one of the Riviera's big family attractions. Few kids are not enchanted by swimming and snorkeling in the coral lagoon, as well as by exploring its lush forest setting.

7 Punta Laguna
MAP N4 ■ daily

Getting to see local wildlife *(see p94)* in its natural habitat, rather than in zoos or nature parks, can take time and effort, but at this small reserve *(see p56)* north of Cobá village guides lead the way and you can see spider monkeys jumping through the trees after just a little exciting exploration. Deer, wild boar, and lots of birds can likely be seen too.

8 Laguna Chankanaab, Cozumel

One of the most enjoyable and accessible places *(see p54)* for even small children to be dazzled by a first introduction to snorkeling and the underwater treasures of the Cozumel reefs. The sea is very placid, and there's coral and abundant sea life just off the beach. There's also a coral lagoon in the same park *(see p14)*.

Children playing at Playa Mia

9 Laguna Yal-Ku, Akumal
MAP P5 ■ Open 8am–6pm daily ■ Adm

This winding rock pool of brilliant turquoise water right at the north end of Akumal's Media Luna Bay is one of the natural coral inlets on the Riviera coast. Rarely crowded, it's delightful for swimming and snorkeling with young children, with coral and colorful fish that are easy to spot.

Rock pool at Laguna Yal-Ku, Akumal

10 Playa Mia, Cozumel
MAP R6 ■ Open dawn–dusk daily ■ Adm

Cozumel's beach clubs offer all the fun of the sand and sea, plus restaurants and loungers in the shade. Playa Mia has the best choice of things to do for older children – snorkeling, beach games, kayaks, and banana boats – and it has a Kids' Club for little ones.

☰⓿ Nightspots

① Señor Frog's, Cancún
MAP L4

As the sun goes down, Señor Frog's *(see p86)* transforms from a restaurant into one of Cancún's most famous nightspots. Daily live music, DJs, and karaoke create an atmosphere in which to dance the night away. Not to be missed is the water slide that runs from the venue to the lagoon, so make sure you come prepared with your swimwear. Open until the early hours of the morning.

Vibrant interior of Señor Frog's

② Mandala, Playa del Carmen

Located in the center of Playa, this chic nightclub *(see p85)* is a favorite of those who wish to party till dawn. The club is set over two floors with an Asian-inspired style and offers a good selection of music.

③ Kin Toh, Tulum
MAP P6 ■ Carretera Tulum-Punta Allen km 5 ■ (984) 980 0640

A great place to begin a night out in Tulum, this quirky spot has several "nests" – round seating areas set at the level of the surrounding tree-tops. Arrive early for stellar sunsets and then enjoy drinks from the excellent cocktail menu.

④ Amma Club, Cancún

This cool club *(see p85)* is famous for its ice bar and has a special area with frozen sculptures that are great for selfies. The club also has a sizeable dance floor where patrons dance to music played by DJs. There are special party nights held throughout the year, too, including an Independence day-themed party in September.

⑤ Dinner Cruises, Cancún
Marina Aquatours (Cancún Lovers): MAP K3; Blvd Kukulcán, km 6.25; (998) 193 3370

For a slightly more sedate time try another Cancún specialty, with live shows, games, dinner, and dancing to live bands as you sail around Laguna Nichupté or to Isla Mujeres. Each one is themed: Cancún Queen from Aqua World *(see p54)* is like an old sternwheeled riverboat, the Cancún Lovers Cruise is on a replica Columbus-era galleon, and Captain Hook's Pirate Night *(see p85)* is, of course, on a pirate ship.

⑥ Carlos'n Charlie's, Cozumel
MAP R5

Enjoyable, crowd-pleasing food and a non-stop, bright and breezy party atmosphere are the keys to the success of the Anderson group's bar-restaurants, found all around Mexico under several jokey names – Carlos'n Charlie's *(see p97)*, Senor Frog's, and El Shrimp Bucket. This Cozumel branch in Punta Langosta mall is one of the biggest.

Carlos'n Charlie's, Cozumel

7 Abolengo, Playa del Carmen

MAP Q4

Fuel up on tasty tacos, then get ready to dance the night away with a cocktail in hand at this colorful spot. The bar is most famous for its neon-themed parties, where bar staff dress in neon outfits, including one in a giant flashing robot costume. Visitors love the varied playlist spun by house DJs.

8 La Fundación Mezcalería, Mérida

MAP C2

Even though the Yucatán is not Mexico's mezcal-producing region like the state of Jalisco, it still specializes in one of Mexico's most iconic spirits. As the bar's name suggests, the smoky agave-based spirit is the specialty here (see p114), and is served in many of its creative cocktails. Expect live music and DJ sets, too.

9 Coco Bongo, Cancún

MAP L4

The most state-of-the-art of all Cancún's mega-clubs, Coco Bongo

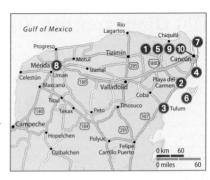

(see p85) is a vast, multilevel, multi-space venue with music that covers all the bases – techno, rock, Latin – from DJs and live bands. There is also a space to eat. House specialties include ultraextravagant theme nights, live shows, and other surprises.

10 Dady'O, Cancún

MAP L4

Always the most popular among American students on spring break, this equally huge venue (see p85) across the street from the Coco Bongo guarantees a noisy, down-home party atmosphere – theme parties are a permanent feature. Next door, the slightly smaller Sweet is a live venue with a bar-restaurant, plus more fun and games.

The exterior of the famed Coco Bongo nightclub in Cancún

TOP 10 Dishes of the Yucatán

Delicious *cochinita pibil*

1 Cochinita Pibil

This punchy dish dates back to pre-Conquest Mayan cooking – pork marinated in lime, bitter orange, and *achiote* (a mild spice with a slightly peppery taste), wrapped in banana leaves and baked in an earthenware dish. A flavorful food, it's very versatile and can be served as a main course or used to fill tacos. *Pollo pibil* is a chicken version of this dish.

2 Puchero

Commonly eaten as a Sunday lunch, *puchero* is a hearty stew found across Latin America, but with its origins in Spain. In the Yucatán Peninsula it is typically packed with pork, beef, chicken, and vegetables, spiced with allspice and cinnamon, and finished off with a garnish of diced habañero peppers, oranges, coriander, and radishes.

3 Poc-Chuc

Marinating is one of the most characteristic skills of Yucatecan cooking, and this delicious dish features pork marinated in the juice of *naranja agria* (small, bitter oranges, special to the region), cooked with onions, herbs, and garlic, and served with black beans. With a wonderful mix of sweet and savory flavors, it's very popular, but debate rages as to whether it is really traditional or a creation of La Chaya Maya restaurant *(see p71)* in Mérida.

4 Pollo Oriental de Valladolid

The pride of Valladolid: chicken quartered on the bone and casseroled with garlic, onion, cloves, and a mix of both hot and mild chilis; it's then quickly roasted in a baste of maize oil and bitter orange juice. This is another regional dish with a rich, densely layered combination of different flavors. *Pavo oriental* is the turkey version.

5 Relleno Negro

Yucatecan cooking likes rich concoctions. In *relleno negro* ("black stuffing"), finely ground pork, peppers, grated hard-boiled egg, herbs, spices, and a powerful combination of chilis are mixed together to make up a thick, majestic sauce. It is usually served with *pavo or guajolote* (turkey), the region's most traditional meat.

Classic *pollo con mole*

6 Pollo con Mole

This dish is a central Mexican classic. Fried chicken is covered in *mole*, a thick, spicy, savory – not at all sweet – chocolate sauce. Richly satisfying, this is one of the oldest uses of chocolate, its flavor uniting perfectly with strongly spiced meats.

7 Crepas de Chaya

Tasting like spinach, *chaya* is a vegetable native to the Yucatán. It features in traditional cooking and contemporary dishes such as this one. It is cooked with garlic and wrapped in light, European-style wheat pancakes (crêpes) and served with a cheese sauce. *Chaya* is also used to make drinks *(see p71)*.

Camarón al mojo de ajo

8 Camarón al Mojo de Ajo

All around the coasts, fish and seafood are restaurant staples. One of the simplest and most delicious ways of cooking the likes of *camarón* (prawns/shrimp) and *caracol* (conch) is *al mojo de ajo*, fried quickly in hot oil and lots of garlic.

9 Sopa de Lima

One of the most popular classics of Yucatecan cooking, "lime soup" is actually made with chicken, boned, chopped into strips, and then slow-cooked with coriander, onions, herbs, spices, and masses of local sweet limes. It's served with strips of dry tortillas for added crunch.

10 Arroz con Pulpo

A Campeche specialty: a delicious warm salad that's much lighter than many local dishes on a hot day. Rice *(arroz)* is mixed together with chopped octopus *(pulpo)*, red peppers, onion, coriander, and other herbs, plus, often, mango, papaya, or other fruits, in a refreshing blend of sweet juice and salty seafood flavors.

TOP 10 YUCATECAN SNACKS AND STREET FOODS

1 Ceviche
Raw fish or seafood marinated in lemon or lime juice, and served with salad, spices, and lots of coriander.

2 Cócteles
Usually, fish or seafood ceviches served in a glass accompanied by a vinaigrette-style dressing.

3 Papadzules
A Mayan dish of chopped hard-boiled eggs in a sweet pumpkin-seed sauce, rolled in tortillas and often served with a spicy tomato sauce.

4 Panuchos
Small, crisp-fried tortillas covered in refried beans and topped with strips of chicken or turkey, plus generous helpings of chopped tomato, onion, avocado, and chilis.

5 Salbutes
Similar to *panuchos*, but made with a thicker, spongier base instead of crisp tortillas.

6 Enchiladas
In southern Mexico, these rolled soft tortillas with various fillings tend to be served with a rich *mole* sauce.

7 Tacos
Small rolled tortillas filled with 1,001 possible fillings: at taco stands, they're served rolled up; at *taquerías* you sit and assemble them yourself.

8 Fajitas
Pan-fried meat or seafood served sizzling alongside bowls of onions, refried beans, chili sauce, guacamole, and soft tortillas.

9 Tortas
Small bread rolls, available with as many different fillings as tacos.

10 Quesadillas
Small, soft tortillas that are folded over and filled with melted cheese and sometimes ham, and served up with a range of sauces.

Stuffed quesadillas

🔟 Restaurants

The colorful exterior of Mexican restaurant La Parrilla in Cancún

① La Habichuela, Cancún

Superb Yucatecan and Mexican cooking, well-presented with original touches, is served in the tranquil setting of a lush garden here *(see p87)*. Campeche dishes include *cocobichuela*, shrimp and lobster in curry sauce served with coconut rice.

② El Marlín Azul, Mérida

It's easy to walk past this seafood restaurant *(see p115)* and miss it. Look for a blue awning and a crowd of regulars perched at the counter – they're enjoying some of the best seafood in the city, trucked in daily direct from Celestún.

③ Los Pelícanos, Puerto Morelos

Set beneath a giant *palapa* palm roof, in a spot above the beach, this easygoing local institution *(see p87)* serves some of the best ceviches you'll find, as well as grander seafood dishes.

④ Kinich, Izamal

Tucked into a secluded garden near the largest of Izamal's Mayan pyramids, this *(see p107)* is the place to sample the full range of Yucatecan cooking – *cochinita*, *pavo en relleno negro*, and a fragrant *sopa de lima*.

⑤ La Parrilla, Cancún

At this restaurant, Mexican art and music create an atmospheric setting for delicious local specialties, including Mayan dishes. The ambience, great food, and affordable prices have turned La Parrilla *(see p87)* into a successful formula exported to other centers along the Riviera.

⑥ Hartwood, Tulum

Everything is cooked over an open fire at this hip restaurant *(see p99)*, run by a former New York restaurateur with a focus on sustainable, eco-friendly cuisine. The tasty, creative menu changes every day, depending on what produce is available and in season.

Outdoor dining at Hartwood, Tulum

⑦ Casa de Piedra, Xcanatún

Yucatecan and Caribbean traditions and ingredients are combined here *(see p115)* with sophisticated international styles by a French-trained chef: a delicate *sopa de lima* is a menu fixture, alongside the chef's own interesting creations, such as cream of *poblano* chili soup with roquefort.

⑧ Ku'uk, Mérida

Set in one of Mérida's grand mansions, Ku'uk *(see p114)* is a worthy splurge with a great value haute cuisine tasting menu. Chef Pedro Evia uses traditional ingredients and local produce to create innovative dishes that make for an unforgettable experience. The regularly changing menu is complemented with sophisticated cocktails.

Interior of La Chaya Maya

⑨ La Chaya Maya, Mérida

A cheerful and very popular restaurant *(see p115)*, specializing in Yucatecan cuisine. Serving staff in traditional Mayan dress serve up local dishes such as *puchero*, *poc-chuc*, and *sopa de lima (see pp68–9)*. There are two branches in the city center.

⑩ La Pigua, Campeche

The best seafood restaurant *(see p99)* in the city offers an attractive dining room, immaculate service, and an appealing menu featuring coconut prawns, octopus in a garlic sauce, and freshly-caught fish in a variety of sauces.

TOP 10 BREAKFASTS AND JUICES

Huevos Motuleños

1 Huevos Motuleños
Like *huevos rancheros*, but with the addition of peas, ham, and grated cheese, often served with slices of fried banana.

2 Huevos Rancheros
A breakfast classic: tortillas topped by fried eggs, covered in spicy tomato sauce, and served with refried beans.

3 Huevos Revueltos
Scrambled eggs, nearly always mixed with a little onion and red pepper, or with ham (*con jamón*).

4 Huevos a la Mexicana
Spicy scrambled eggs with peppers, chili, chopped onions, and chorizo.

5 Chilaquiles
Crisp tortilla chips, baked in a cheese sauce with tomato, onions, herbs, chili, and shredded chicken or turkey.

6 Platillo de Fruta
A big plate of fresh fruit, usually including at least pineapple, watermelon, oranges, bananas, and papaya.

7 Agua de Jamaica
An enormously refreshing local product – an infusion of dried flowers of jamaica (a kind of hibiscus), diluted to make a delicious tall drink.

8 Agua de Chaya
Another infusion, this one of the vegetable *chaya (see p69)*, best mixed with water and a little squeeze of lemon juice.

9 Licuados
Any kind of fruit, such as watermelon, papaya, pineapple, or mamey, pulped and diluted with water and ice.

10 Raspados
Vibrant fruit juices with crushed ice, packed right to the top of the glass.

🔟 Cancún and the Yucatán for Free

① Nightlife in Mérida
MAP C2

Each night of the week the city center plays host to a range of live music, dance events, theatrical performances, film screenings, and other entertainment. Check out the latest schedule at the city's (see pp32–3) tourist office.

② MACAY, Mérida
MAP C2 ■ Pasaje de la Revolución ■ Open 10am–2pm Mon, Tue, Thu–Sat ■ www.macay.org

The Museo de Arte Contemporáneo Ateneo de Yucatán (MACAY) in Mérida (see pp32–3) is home to an outstanding modern art collection, featuring works by leading Yucatecán painters such as Fernando Castro Pacheco and Fernando García Ponce.

③ Palacio Centro Cultural, Campeche

Charting the tempestuous history of Campeche (see pp38–9), this museum offers multimedia displays and innovative exhibits, including a replica Spanish galleon. Most of the descriptions are in Spanish, with a few also in English. There's also a spectacular music and light show on weekends.

San Bernardino Sisal altarpiece

④ San Bernardino Sisal, Valladolid

An elegant Franciscan church (see p46) and former convent San Bernardino Sisal has a magnificent 18th-century altarpiece, as well as walls that are covered with evocative 17th-century paintings.

⑤ Izamal's Crafts Workshops
MAP D2 ■ Various locations around town ■ Most workshops open from around 10am–2pm & 4–7pm daily

The small town of Izamal (see p103) is famous for its spectacular crafts scene, and its wood-carvers, jewelers, hammock-makers, and other artisans are happy to show tourists round their workshops (see p105). A map showing the locations of many such workshops is available from most hotels in town for free.

Palacio Centro Cultural, Campeche

6 Xlapak
MAP C4

The smallest and least visited of the Ruta Puuc archaeological sites, the Mayan site of Xlapak *(see p112)* features a restored palace with doorways decorated with large, eye-catching Chac (the rain god) masks.

7 Oxkutzcab Market
MAP C4 ■ From 7am daily

This charming colonial-era town, surrounded by fruit and vegetable farms, hosts in its main square one of the liveliest and most colorful markets in the region.

8 Punta Bete Beach
MAP R4

This is one of the most picturesque stretches of sand *(see p62)* on the Riviera Maya, and less crowded than many of its neighbors thanks to a bumpy access road.

Yucatán Carnival performers

9 Carnival

Although it's not quite on the scale of its more famous Brazilian counterpart, carnival *(see p74)* in Mexico is still a lively and raucous affair. Cancún, Cozumel, and Mérida host the biggest celebrations in the Yucatán region – expect costumed dancers, live music, and plenty of good food and drink. Carnival takes place in the week before Lent.

10 Mérida Cathedral
MAP C2

Dating back to the late 16th century, Mérida's *(see pp32–3)* imposing cathedral is one of the oldest in Latin America.

TOP 10 BUDGET TIPS

Fried tortillas at a food stall

1 Markets and snack stands are the cheapest and often the most atmospheric places to eat.

2 Visit in the low-season: May–June and late November–early December offer the best combinations of prices and weather.

3 The extensive public bus system is an inexpensive way to travel around.

4 It is cheaper to rent a car at a small agency in Mérida than in Cancún.

5 Local free magazines often have discount coupons for hotels, restaurants, and other attractions.

6 Some national monuments offer free admission for Mexican nationals on Sundays, and general admission to museums and historic sites is generally cheaper for Mexican residents.

7 Many ticket-based attractions (except Mayan sites) offer discounts for booking online in advance.

8 Most diving operators offer discounts for group or advance bookings, or if you book several dives at the same time.

9 Most Riviera Maya bars offer two- for-one deals for at least a few hours each night.

10 Save money by using pesos rather than US dollars.

Mexican currency

Festivals

① Feast of Three Kings, Tizimín

MAP F2 ■ **Two weeks from Jan 6**

The capital of Yucatán's cattle country hosts one of the region's biggest fiestas featuring a stock fair with traditional music, dancing, colorful parades, and plenty of eating and drinking.

② La Candelaria

MAP E3 ■ **12 days around Feb 2**

Valladolid's main fiesta, Expo-Feria centers around the Feast of the Virgin of La Candelaria. Local girls show off dazzling embroidered dresses in the opening parade, followed by dancing and free concerts and shows. Campeche has a smaller celebration.

③ Carnival

About one week before Lent

This is the biggest and brightest celebration of the year in the Yucatán. In Cancún and Cozumel the streets fill with music, dancing, food stands, and a little Río-style parading. The biggest Carnival in southern Mexico, though, is in Mérida.

④ Equinoxes, Chichén Itzá and Dzibilchaltún

Mar 21 & Sep 21

The visual effects integral to these Mayan cities – such as the "descent" of the sun down the serpents on El Castillo at Chichén and the striking of the rising sun through the Seven Dolls temple at Dzibilchaltún – were timed to happen on the spring and fall equinoxes. Today, some 80,000 visit Chichén Itzá (see p29) for the day; the crowds are smaller at Dzibilchaltún (see p110).

⑤ San Miguel Arcángel, Cozumel

MAP H3–4 ■ **Sep 20–29**

Cozumel's most important traditional fiesta takes place in honor of the island's patron saint, St. Michael. Over the nine days that precede his feast day, religious processions are held in town, and there's entertainment for children, plus free music and dancing.

Performance at Cancún Jazz Festival

⑥ Cancún Jazz Festival

Check website for festival dates ■ **www.musicgetaways.com**

A mix of young artists from Latin America, the U.S., and Europe – often playing Latin Jazz and contemporary fusion rather than strict jazz – features in this festival. Several acts play for free in Parque de las Palapas in Ciudad Cancún.

Equinox at Chichén Itza

⑦ Cristo de las Ampollas, Mérida

MAP C2 ▪ Week before Oct 13

More solemnly religious than most fiestas, with processions culminating on October 13, when the figure of "Christ of the Blisters" (*Cristo de las Ampollas*), kept in Mérida Cathedral, is carried through town before a Mass.

Day of the Dead sugar skulls for sale

⑧ Day of the Dead and All Saints' Day

Oct 31–Nov 2

Sugar skulls, dead bread (*pan de muerto*), zempazuchitl flowers, and coffin-shaped decorations are the mark of Mexico's most famous celebration, when people party to honor the dead on Halloween and All Saints' Day (*Todos Santos*), and families visit cemeteries to picnic by the graves of their departed relatives.

⑨ Mérida en Domingo

MAP C2 ▪ Every Sun

Every week, Mérida hosts a free fiesta, "Mérida on Sunday," when the Plaza Mayor and Calle 60 are closed to traffic to make way for strolling crowds and a range of events. There are displays of *jarana* dancing in front of the City Hall and concerts up and down the street, and anyone can dance.

⑩ Village Fiestas

Every village and town in the Yucatán also has its own fiesta, when the streets are covered in bright garlands, work ceases, and music is heard non-stop. To find out if and when any are due to take place near you, ask in tourist offices, look out for posters, or check local papers.

TOP 10 TRADITIONAL CRAFTS AND PRODUCTS

1 Ceramics
Huge numbers of earthenware pots are made in Ticul, sometimes using pre-Conquest techniques.

2 Embroidery
Lush flower designs are made by Mayan women on traditional *huípil* blouses, handkerchiefs, tablecloths, and other linen.

3 Panama Hats
The best palm hats are said to be from northern Campeche, and the place to buy them is Mérida.

4 Guayaberas
These are light, elegant shirts. They are accepted as tropical formal wear and bestow instant dignity upon men (of any age).

5 Sandals
Huge racks of traditional leather *huarache* sandals can be found in all Yucatán markets.

6 Wood Carving
Many Mayan villagers carve wooden figures based on ancient images.

7 *Jícaras* (Gourds)
Dried natural gourd bowls, brightly painted, are a specialty of Chiapas, but they are often seen in the Yucatán.

8 Silverwork and Jewelry
Fine silverware from Taxco in central Mexico is found in Yucatán stores, as well as amber from Chiapas.

9 Painted Birds and Ornaments
Brightly painted wooden parrots, toucans, and boxes provide some of the prettiest images of tropical Mexico.

10 Hammocks
The traditional place to sleep is so much a part of the Yucatán that local poets have even celebrated it in verse.

Colorful hammocks for sale

Cancún and the Yucatán Area by Area

The Mayan temple-pyramid, El Castillo, overlooking Tulum's lovely beaches

Cancún and the North	**78**
Cozumel and the South	**90**
The Central Heartland	**100**
The West	**108**

TOP 10 Cancún and the North

Cancún is the great magnet at the top of the Mayan Riviera, with lavish hotels, shopping and dining of every kind, wild nightclubs, theme parks, water parks, and other entertainment spread out along one of the world's finest beaches. To the south is Playa del Carmen, a trendier, more compact vacation town, and family-friendly eco-parks that provide an unforgettable introduction to the nature of tropical Yucatán. For a change from resort life, in the same area there are also places where the frenetic pace of modern life still seems delightfully far away – in the ever-mellow Puerto Morelos, at the spectacular bird reserve on Isla Contoy, and on the lovely Isla Mujeres.

Leopard, Xcaret

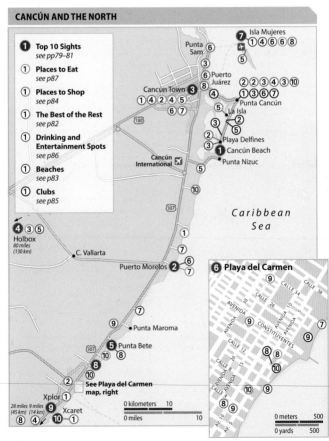

CANCÚN AND THE NORTH

1 **Top 10 Sights**
see pp79–81

1 **Places to Eat**
see p87

1 **Places to Shop**
see p84

1 **The Best of the Rest**
see p82

1 **Drinking and Entertainment Spots**
see p86

1 **Beaches**
see p83

1 **Clubs**
see p85

Holbox
80 miles
(130 km)

C. Vallarta

Puerto Morelos

Punta Maroma

Punta Bete

Xplor
28 miles 9 miles
(45 km) (14 km)

Xcaret

See Playa del Carmen map, right

Isla Mujeres

Punta Sam

Puerto Juárez

Cancún Town

La Isla

Punta Cancún

Playa Delfines

Cancún Beach

Punta Nizuc

Cancún International

Caribbean Sea

6 **Playa del Carmen**

CALLE 38
CALLE 34
CALLE 26
AVENIDA
CONSTITUYENTES
CALLE 12
CALLE 8
AVENIDA
AV. 10
AV. 5

0 kilometers   10
0 miles   10

0 meters   500
0 yards   500

The white-sand arc and azure waters at Cancún Beach

1 Cancún Beach
MAP L4–K6

Every one of the Riviera's beaches has the same wonderful fine white sand, which stays deliciously cool to the touch, but Cancún's is unquestionably the finest, stretching the whole 14 miles (23 km) of Cancún Island. Along it, in the Hotel Zone, are resort hotels, shopping and entertainment centers, watersports and snorkeling, and fun parks, plus the Mayan site of El Rey (see pp12–13).

Puerto Morelos

2 Puerto Morelos
MAP R3

This little fishing town was the biggest place on this coast before the rise of Cancún. It has avoided overdevelopment and retains a low-key atmosphere, much loved by the many foreigners who own houses here or stay whole winters in its small hotels. There's a beautiful white beach, and a superb reef close offshore, now protected as a marine park. Local dive operators and fishing guides give individual, friendly service.

3 Cancún Town
MAP J3

On the mainland at the north end of Cancún Island, Ciudad Cancún (see pp12–13), also known as "Downtown," was created at the same time as the Hotel Zone in the 1970s. It has developed an atmosphere of its own, though, and the main drag of Avenida Tulum and the nearby squares and avenues are enjoyable places to explore, with plenty of shopping and great restaurants.

4 Isla Holbox
MAP G1 ■ Passenger ferry from Chiquilá: 6am–9:30pm daily ■ www.holboxisland.com

This tiny peninsula (see p63) is one of the Yucatán's hippest destinations. Set beside a wide lagoon filled with birds and dolphins, and accessed by a 15-minute ferry journey, Holbox is a wonderfully relaxed village whose sandy streets are lined with small hotels and restaurants. There's a vast beach and, in season, the waters offshore are temporarily home to migrating whale sharks.

5 Punta Bete
MAP R4

Often unnoticed (see p83) between Puerto Morelos and Playa del Carmen, and kept off the beaten track by a bumpy 2-mile (3-km) access road through the jungle, this point (see p62) is flanked by lines of palm-fringed bays – perfect arcs of dazzling white sand by a turquoise sea. They are shared by a few resort hotels, and far more small-scale, cheaper clusters of beach cabañas.

THE CHICLE BOOM

Long before tourism, this region's biggest business was chewing gum. When gum was first invented in the 19th century it was all made with natural chicle, found in the wild sapodilla trees of the Yucatán. Villages such as Puerto Juárez and Puerto Morelos were all founded as harbors for exporting chicle, brought in by sapodilla-tappers, who roamed the forests inland.

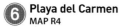

Shops at Playa del Carmen

⑥ Playa del Carmen
MAP R4

The Riviera's most vibrant street life, by day and night, and its hippest crowds can be found in this resort town *(see pp16–17)*. Playa's long-established cool bars and backpackers' haunts mix with modern hotels ranging from big resorts to cozy guesthouses. As well as having wonderful beaches, it's great for diving and snorkeling.

⑦ Isla Mujeres
MAP L1–2

Although it's only a short ferry ride away from Cancún, this 5-mile (8-km) long island *(see pp20–21)*, the first place where Spaniards landed in Mexico in 1517, has a very different atmosphere, with few big hotels,

one small town, a good choice of inexpensive places to stay, and a relaxed beach-town feel. Isla Mujeres is also an excellent diving, snorkeling, and fishing center, with an exciting range of reefs to explore offshore.

⑧ Isla Contoy
MAP H1

Mexico's most important sea-bird reserve covers the whole of this uninhabited island *(see pp20–21)*. The terrain is a mix of mangroves, beaches, and coral lagoons that are home to over 50 species of birds – they contain turtle breeding grounds too. Day tours are offered by dive shops on Isla Mujeres *(see p56)*.

⑨ Xplor
MAP Q4 ■ Federal Highway 307, km 282 ■ (998) 883 3143 ■ Open 9am–5pm Mon–Fri (until 8pm weekends) ■ Adm ■ www.xplor.travel

A trip to Xplor *(see pp54–5)* is the ideal day out, which the whole family can enjoy.

Isla Mujeres beachfront

Seven different circuits await, including 14 ziplines; two 3-mile (5-km) long amphibious vehicle paths, running along jungle tracks, over rope bridges and through caves; two underground river-raft circuits; and the chance to swim along a subterranean river amongst amazing rock formations.

River-rafting in Xplor

 Xcaret
MAP Q4

The largest of the Riviera's growing number of eco-parks (see pp18–19), just south of Playa del Carmen, this provides a wonderful introduction to the tropical environment of the Yucatán. There's a full day's worth of things to do – from snorkeling and swimming to watching a fascinating collection of animals and butterflies.

CANCÚN TO TULUM

▶ DAY ONE

Begin by exploring the more traditional side of Cancún with a *desayuno* at one of the **Mercado 28 restaurants** (see p87), in the town market. Then rent a car and drive south through the Hotel Zone along Boulevard Kukulcán.

Call in at Gran Museo del Mundo Maya (see p12) and the atmospheric **El Rey** site (see p82). Stop off at **Playa Delfines** (see p83), for crashing surf and a spectacular view back along Cancún Island.

Pause at **Puerto Moreles** (see p79) for a lunch of seafood ceviche and a cool beer at **Los Pelícanos** (see p87), watching the pelicans hang in the breeze. After snorkeling over Puerto's reef, continue on to **Playa del Carmen**. Check out the beach and the shops on Quinta Avenida. As darkness falls, join the strolling crowds along the Quinta.

DAY TWO

After breakfast, continue south towards **Tulum** (see pp22–3). Your route will take you past **Xplor** and **Xcaret**, as well as the glamorous vacation spot of **Puerto Aventuras** (see p91), and the gorgeous beaches of **Xpu-Ha** (see p93) and **Akumal** (see p92). In Akumal, have lunch at **Tequilaville** (see p99). On arrival in Tulum, take time to explore the cliff-top Mayan site, then spend the rest of the day swimming and sunbathing on the beach, before enjoying dinner cooked over at open fire at **Hartwood** (see p99).

See map on p78 ←

The Best of the Rest

1 Playacar
MAP Q4

The plusher side *(see p60)* of Playa del Carmen, with a fascinating jungle aviary in the midst of landscaped avenues lined with big resort hotels and private villas.

2 El Rey Site, Cancún
MAP K5 ■ Open 9am–4:30pm daily ■ Adm

This was a relatively small Mayan city, but its layout, with a clearly visible "main street," makes it easy to imagine people bustling about, buying and selling.

The atmospheric El Rey Site

3 El Meco Site, Cancún
MAP K2 ■ Open 8am–4pm daily ■ Adm

The remains of an important Mayan city, were probably founded here in about 300 CE. They feature impressive carvings of animals and monsters.

4 Cenote Kantun-Chi
MAP P5 ■ Open 9am–5pm daily ■ Adm ■ www.kantunchi.com

Visitors can enjoy a revitalizing swim in the cenote's clear, freshwater pool *(see p54)*. There is also a beautiful underground cavern to explore.

5 Ventura Park, Cancún
MAP J6 ■ Blvd Kukulcán, km 25 ■ (998) 881 3035 ■ Open 10am–5pm daily ■ Adm ■ www.venturapark.com

With a 350-yard (320-m) lazy river and a water park, this *(see p54)* park is the biggest of its kind in the Riviera.

6 Puerto Juárez and Punta Sam
MAP K1–2

The little passenger (Puerto Juárez) and car (Punta Sam) ferry ports for Isla Mujeres *(see pp20–21)* are older than any other part of Cancún.

7 Acamaya
MAP R3

A secluded spot perfect for getting away from just about everything, Acamaya is set at the end of the bumpy beach road north from Puerto Morelos. There's a small cabaña hotel and a camping site.

8 Xcacel Beach
MAP P6 ■ Xcacel 504, 77533 Cancún ■ Adm

Lined by lush forest on one side and ocean on the other, the white-sand Xcacel Beach *(see p82)* brims with natural beauty. It's also one of the places that help conservation efforts to protect endangered sea turtles.

9 Punta Maroma
MAP R4

Among the palm-fringed bays at Punta Maroma are several reserved exclusively for guests at the luxurious Maroma retreat *(see p128)*.

10 Moon Palace

One of the largest and best equipped of the Riviera's resorts, the Moon Palace *(see p128)* is set in its own area of jungle to the south of Cancún.

The beautiful Moon Palace resort

Beaches

Visitors relaxing on the popular Playa Norte beach, Isla Mujeres

1 Playa Norte, Isla Mujeres
MAP L1

The beach bums' favorite on Isla, this compact strip of white sand has plenty to keep you entertained, from pedalos, kayaks, and snorkeling to great bars under the palms.

2 Playa Gaviota Azul, Cancún
MAP L4 ▪ Blvd Kukulcán, km 9

One of the best beaches on the east side, and located in the party-ing center, Playa Gaviota Azul is the perfect place for after-party relaxation. Adjacent is the City Beach Club.

3 Playa Delfines, Cancún
MAP K5 ▪ Blvd Kukulcán, km 18

A great place to find space to stretch out, with huge banks of white sand above pounding ocean surf. There's an amazing view north along the beachscape of Cancún Island.

4 Playa Secreto, Isla Mujeres
MAP L1

This broad, sheltered, shallow inlet tucked away from the main North Beach is especially good for small kids. Its waters are always tranquil, and the beach is rarely crowded.

5 Isla Holbox
MAP G1

For lovers of real seclusion, with miles of beach from which to pick a spot that's just right. The island (see p79) faces the opal waters of the Gulf of Mexico, however, so there's no coral.

6 Puerto Morelos
MAP R3

Excellent for carefree swimming, Puerto Morelos (see p79) has not only fine, uncrowded white sands, but also a reef full of vivid underwater life just offshore.

7 Playa del Secreto
MAP R4

A short way south of Puerto Morelos, this big, broad, white-sand beach is mostly fronted by private villas, with scarcely any hotels, so there's never any shortage of space.

8 Punta Bete
MAP R4

One (see p79) of the most beautiful spots on the whole Riviera – palms, white-sand bays, and turquoise sea. A terrible access road helps keep it that way.

9 Playa del Carmen
MAP Q4

Playa's main town beach (see pp16–17) is the place to go to survey other sun worshipers, and to show-case your skills at beach volleyball and other seaside pursuits.

10 Chunzubul, Playa del Carmen
MAP Q4

Keep walking along the beach north from Playa to find endless space, the best snorkeling and diving spots, and nudist beaches (see pp120–21). It is safest to avoid leaving bags unat-tended in the really quiet spots.

See map on p78

Places to Shop

1 La Casa del Arte Mexicano, Cancún

MAP K3 ■ Blvd Kukulcán, km 4

The gift shop at this folk-art museum, in the grounds of Xcaret, stocks high-quality crafts from all over Mexico, including some fun toys.

2 Forum by the Sea, Cancún

MAP K4 ■ Blvd Kukulcán, km 9.5 ■ Open 10am–midnight daily

Highlights here are perfume and jewelry stores and brands such as Harley Davidson and Zingara. It also has a huge Hard Rock at its center.

3 Coral Negro, Cancún

MAP L4 ■ Boulevard Kukulcán, km 9.5

A rambling jewelry and handicrafts bazaar a few steps from the Forum. You can find fine traditional craft-work here, as well as a lot of junk.

4 Plaza Caracol, Cancún

MAP K4 ■ Blvd Kukulcán, km 8.5

One of the biggest and most varied of the Cancún malls, with engaging toy shops, beachwear, fine jewelry, and a huge choice of restaurants in an attractive, light-filled building.

5 La Isla, Cancún

MAP K4 ■ Blvd Kukulcán, km 12.5

One of the most stylish of the Hotel Zone's malls, built as an artificial island surrounded by Venetian-style "canals." It's the place for top names such as Hugo Boss, Diesel, and Zara.

6 Mercado 23, Cancún

MAP J3 ■ Off Avenida Tulum, on Calle Cedro

This colorful little open-air market is where locals go to shop for meat, vegetables, herbal cures, and even party supplies and piñatas.

7 Mercado 28, Cancún

MAP J3 ■ Av Xel-Ha and Av Tankah

The town market *(see p87)* offers old-style shopping with stands of *huarache* sandals and panama hats, and tables full of fresh vegetables and fruit – plus a great food court.

8 Avenida Hidalgo, Isla Mujeres Town

MAP L1

This is Isla's main street, and its main drag for leisurely browsing. Here and in parallel Av Juárez small shops offer painted wooden birds, and local shell and coral jewelry.

9 Super Telas, Playa del Carmen

MAP Q4 ■ Constituyentes, Plaza Las Perlas

Fine quality Mexican textiles *(telas)*, in traditional or original designs, can be found in this original shop.

10 Caracol, Playa del Carmen

MAP Q4 ■ Av 5, from Calle 6 to 84

The specialties at this two-story boutique are textiles and embroidery from all over Mexico – particularly Chiapas – and from Guatemala.

The canalside stores of La Isla, Cancún

Clubs

1 Coco Bongo, Cancún
MAP L4 ■ Blvd Kukulcán, km 9.5 ■ (998) 883 5061 ■ Open from 10:30pm daily ■ Adm

Cancún's most high-powered, high-tech, multilevel mega-club (see p67), Coco Bongo has a wide-ranging menu of music options.

Crowd partying at Coco Bongo

2 Amma Club
MAP K4 ■ Blvd Kukulcán, km 12.7 ■ (998) 223 4656 ■ Open 11pm–6am Fri–Sat ■ Adm

In steamy Yucatán, this ice bar has ski goggle and anorak-wearing bartenders shaking up frosty cocktails while DJs spin reggaeton and house music.

3 Chicabal Sunset Club
MAP K5 ■ Blvd Kukulcán, Marina del Rey ■ (998) 385 1099 ■ Open 1–7pm Thu–Sun ■ Adm

Situated on a private beach, this stylish club hosts pool parties and offers beautiful ocean views.

4 Captain Hook's Pirate Night, Cancún
MAP K3 ■ El Embarcadero, Blvd Kukulcán, km 4.5 ■ (998) 849 4452 ■ Check in 6:30pm daily ■ Adm

Dinner cruises are normally more sedate than clubbing in Cancún, but Captain Hook's (see p66), with its "pirate crew," is pretty boisterous.

5 La Casa del Hábano
MAP K4 ■ Blvd Kukulcán, km 12.7 ■ (998) 840 7000 ■ Open 10am–9pm daily

With its wood paneled walls and leather chairs, this place has a refined yet relaxed air. Along with selling a range of Cuban cigars, from Cohibas to Macanudos, the bar here serves up some of the best mojitos in town.

6 Cun Crawl, Cancún
MAP L4 ■ Blvd Kukulcán, km 9.5 ■ (998) 165 0699

Chill out in the lounge area, or hit the dance floor, as the DJs mix and play creative blends of European music at this chic nightclub.

7 The City, Cancún
MAP L4 ■ Blvd Kukulcán, km 9.5 ■ (998) 848 8385 (ext 115) ■ Nightclub open from 10pm daily ■ Casual dress but no sandals or bathing suits ■ Adm

This huge, modern nightclub also includes a beach club, restaurant, bar, and lounge.

8 Mandala, Playa del Carmen
MAP H3 ■ Calle 12 Av ■ (998) 883 3333 ■ Open 10pm–4am daily

An Asian-inspired club, Mandala (see p66) is massive, and fills up quickly on the weekends. Bottle service is available.

9 Coralina Daylight Club
MAP H3 ■ Calle 26 ■ (984) 204 6009 ■ Open 11am–7pm Tue–Sun

Coralina capitalizes on the Caribbean sun and sand and its enviable beachside location to attract partygoers long before the sun goes down.

10 La Vaquita, Playa del Carmen
MAP Q4 ■ Calle 12 Norte ■ (998) 848 8380 ■ Open 11pm–6am daily ■ Adm

This lively nightclub, whose name means "Little Cow," is anything but pastoral, and has a man dressed as a cow, offering shots to the crowds.

See map on p78

Drinking and Entertainment Spots

1 Hunter Bar
MAP J3 ■ Alcatraces 45 Mz. 10 Lt. 26 SM 22, Centro

Enjoy cocktails and vegan food under the fairy lights at this bar. There's also karaoke on Wednesdays with a live band, welcome hammocks, and a pool to relax.

The quirky cave setting of Alux

2 Alux, Playa del Carmen
MAP Q4 ■ Av Juaréz 217 ■ $$

This restaurant-bar has the most unusual setting in Playa: an atmospheric cave. It is a good spot for an evening drink or dinner, though prices are a little high. Later in the night, dance to DJs or live jazz.

3 Señor Frog's, Cancún
MAP L4 ■ Blvd Kukulcán, km 9.5

Beside Laguna Nichupté, this *(see p66)* is one of the most popular Cancún outlets of the Anderson group. Party atmosphere, often with rock bands, guaranteed.

4 El Pabilo, Cancún
MAP J3 ■ Av Yaxchilán 31

This cozy café, with a Bohemian feel, offers a welcome respite from loud nightclubs. Live music by local musicians and Cuban expats on weekends.

5 Lola Valentina, Isla Mujeres
MAP L1 ■ Av Miguel Hidalgo

With a bit of everything, Lola Valentina offers breakfast smoothies and a cocktail menu featuring more than ten margaritas, including chipotle and sriracha. Only cash is accepted here.

6 El Café Cito, Isla Mujeres
MAP L1 ■ Av Juárez, corner of Av Matamoros, Isla Town

This mellow place, a few streets from the beach, offers excellent breakfasts and superior coffee, and fresh juice combos later in the day.

7 La Cueva del Chango Restaurante and Bar
MAP Q4 ■ Calle 38 between 5ta Av and El Mar

With its leafy patio, this place feels like a magical secret garden. House cocktails feature combinations such as the Manatí, which blends passionfruit, plantain, and basil with mezcal.

8 Rakata, Playa del Carmen
MAP Q4 ■ Calle 12 Norte

Urban Latin music and reggaeton dominate this club, which bills itself as Cancún's wildest. It hosts occasional dance contests where clubgoers can show off their dance skills.

9 Pez Vela, Playa del Carmen
MAP Q4 ■ Av 5, by Calle 2

Ever popular bar-restaurant with a huge outside terrace that's a fixture on the Quinta Avenida promenade. The style is hippy-Caribbean, helped along by reggae and rock bands.

10 Abolengo
MAP L4 ■ Blvd. Kulkulcán km 9.5

This bar is best known for its "neon parties," featuring neon lights and neon-clad servers. Expect great food and an impressive cocktail menu along with a diverse music selection.

Places to Eat

PRICE CATEGORIES

For a three-course meal for one with a beer or soda (or equivalent meal), taxes and extra charges.

$ under $15 $$ $15–$35 $$$ over $35

1 Le Chique, Cancún

MAP R3 ▪ Puerto Morelos, km 27.5 ▪ (998) 872 8450 ▪ $$$

With classic dishes, such as *cochinita pibil* (see p68), appealing to the palate and the eye, Le Chique is a perfect place to celebrate special occasions.

2 La Habichuela, Cancún

MAP J3 ▪ Calle Margaritas 25 ▪ (998) 840 6240 ▪ $$$

A specialist in Yucatecan and Mexican tropical seafood, this restaurant (see p70) is set in a softly lit garden by the tranquil Parque de las Palapas.

3 El Chapulim, Isla Holbox

MAP G1 ▪ Av Tiburón Ballena ▪ $$

Don't let the lack of a menu deter you from trying out this bistro, which has the best fresh seafood in town and over 25 varieties of Mexican beer.

4 La Parrilla, Cancún

MAP J3 ▪ Av Yaxchilán 51 ▪ (998) 193 3973 ▪ $$

With daily mariachi music creating a warm atmosphere, La Parrilla (see p70) offers a good range of Mexican favorites such as grilled meats, soups, and fondues.

Grilled platters, La Parrilla

5 Mercado 28 Restaurants, Cancún

MAP J3 ▪ Av Xel-Ha and Av Tankah ▪ No credit cards ▪ $

The courtyard of the town market is packed with canopied tables spilling out from restaurants. The traditional food served, such as *pollo con mole* (see p68), is fun and cheap.

6 North Garden

MAP L1 ▪ Carlos Lazo 14, Centro ▪ www.northgarden.com.mx ▪ $$

The dishes here are based around locally farmed ingredients. Try the seafood canoe: baked pineapple stuffed with fish and seafood.

7 Los Pelícanos, Puerto Morelos

MAP R3 ▪ On the Plaza ▪ $$

Linger over the renowned seafood cocktails or one of the subtle fish dishes at one (see p70) of the all-time best beach-terrace restaurants.

8 Lola Rooftop Restaurant, Playa del Carmen

MAP Q4 ▪ Acceso Xcalacoco s/n, Fraccionamiento El Limonar 1 ▪ www.thefiveshotels.com.mx ▪ $$

Inside The Fives Hotel, this rooftop restaurant offers a great view of Playa del Carmen. Pick mezze plates to enjoy Mediterranean-inspired dishes.

9 Los Aguachiles, Playa del Carmen

MAP Q4 ▪ Corner of Calle 34 and Av 25 ▪ $

A low-key open-air snack joint, this place offers an array of delicious tacos and tostadas and an even larger selection of salsas and condiments with which to personalize them.

10 Las Brisas, Playa del Carmen

MAP Q4 ▪ Carretera Federal Cancún, Playa del Carmen ▪ $$$

This big terrace-restaurant has a simple style, but its fresh local seafood is some of the best in town.

See map on p78

⭐ Cozumel and the South

The southern stretch of the Riviera is the less publicized, less built-up part of this coast, but it still offers the choice between luxury resorts and out-of-the-way places – except that here the resorts are not so hectic, and the untouched corners are more remote. Offshore, Cozumel is a relaxing island that offers fabulous diving opportunities. Onshore are some of the Caribbean's most dazzling tropical beaches, such as the seven bays of Xpu-Ha and the crescent of Media Luna Bay. They lead down the coast to the great beach refuge of Tulum, with its Mayan temple sites. A little way inland is another massive Mayan site, the forest-clad city of Cobá.

Sombrero

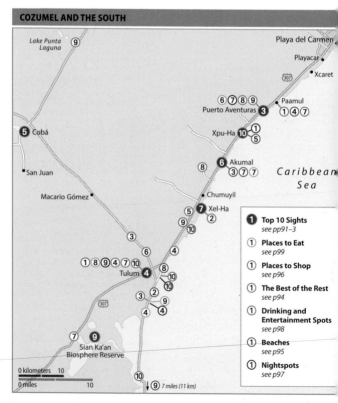

COZUMEL AND THE SOUTH

Lake Punta Laguna ⑨

Playa del Carmen

Playacar

Xcaret

307

⑥⑦⑧⑨ • Paamul
Puerto Aventuras ❸ ①④⑦

⑤ Cobá

Xpu-Ha ⑩ ①⑤

⑧ ❻ Akumal
③⑦⑦

• San Juan

Caribbean Sea

Macario Gómez •

• Chumuyil

⑤ ❼ Xel-Ha
⑨ ②
⑩

❸

⑥ ④

①①⑧⑨④⑦⑩ ❹ Tulum
⑧
⑩
⑩

③ ②
④ ④
307 ⑨

⑦ ⑨
Sian Ka'an
Biosphere Reserve

0 kilometers 10
0 miles 10

⑩
⑨ 7 miles (11 km)

❶	**Top 10 Sights** see pp91–3
①	**Places to Eat** see p99
①	**Places to Shop** see p96
①	**The Best of the Rest** see p94
①	**Drinking and Entertainment Spots** see p98
①	**Beaches** see p95
①	**Nightspots** see p97

Previous pages *Old San Antonio Franciscan monastery in Izamal*

1 Cozumel
MAP R5

Gleaming jewelry stores along the waterfront in San Miguel combine with an easy-going, small-town charm that has long made this island a favorite with families. Cozumel *(see pp14–15)* is a great place to settle into at a leisurely pace, maybe going diving one day, then exploring a little the next: around the island are Mayan sites, windblown cliffs, a fascinating natural wildlife park at Punta Sur, and lovely beaches and snorkeling spots on the west coast.

2 San Gervasio, Cozumel
MAP R5 ▪ (998) 849 2885
▪ Open 8am–5pm daily ▪ Adm

The remains of the Mayan capital *(see p15)* of Cozumel, seized by Cortés and his Spanish soldiers in 1519, are in the middle of the island. Its buildings are small compared to those of the great Mayan cities, but there are many of them – and discovering them, through woods full of wonderful scents, flowers, and birds, involves a lovely walk.

3 Puerto Aventuras
MAP Q5

Puerto Aventuras *(see p21)* is the biggest, most opulent resort on the southern Riviera, a specially created vacation village around an inlet that's now a pretty pleasure port lined with shops and restaurants. The nine-hole golf course is attractive, and the marina is the best-equipped on the whole Riviera, making it a popular base for serious deep-sea fishing enthusiasts. You can take a dip in another part of the harbor.

The clifftop site at Tulum

4 Tulum
MAP P6

Home to a Mayan city perched up on a clifftop, a 7-mile (11-km) palm-fringed beach, and an array of inventive restaurants and boutique hotels, Tulum *(see pp58–9)* is one of the region's most attractive destinations, particularly popular with independent travelers looking for a quieter spot than Playa or Cancún. There's good fishing and diving offshore, and the area around is dotted with beautiful cenotes to explore.

Visitors at the pyramid at Cobá

5 Cobá
MAP M5 ▪ Open 8am–5pm daily ▪ Adm ▪ www.inah.gob.mx

This huge Mayan city (see p45) was once home to around 50,000 people and was the great rival of Chichén Itzá. It's a very different place to visit – it's spread out around several large lakes, and to find its massive buildings you follow fascinating walks through thick forest full of birds. Yucatán's tallest pyramid is here.

6 Akumal
MAP P5

Long a favorite dive destination, with fabulous reefs and places for cave diving, Akumal has grown a good deal without being overwhelmed. It spreads over several long, lovely bays – Media Luna is the most beautiful, with the delightful Yal-Ku lagoon (see p65). There are more apartments, villas, and small hotels than big developments. The beaches near Akumal village are favorite turtle breeding grounds.

7 Xel-Ha
MAP P6 ▪ (998) 251 6560 ▪ Open 8:30am–7pm daily ▪ Adm ▪ www.xelha.com

One of the most luxuriant coral inlets on the coast has been made into a "snorkel park" that's one of the Riviera's most popular attractions – experienced divers may find it tame, but the easy snorkeling is great for families. Around it is a forest park and a beach. Just outside the park and across the highway is the Mayan site of Xel-Ha (see p94).

8 The Cozumel Reefs
Cozumel's greatest glory is its 20-plus coral reefs, an awe-inspiring undersea world of caves, canyons, and

A variety of sealife amid the vibrant coral at the Cozumel Reefs

coral "forests" teeming with life, from sea cucumbers and brilliantly luminous angelfish to graceful rays and the occasional shark. The water is almost perfectly clear and Chankanaab and Paraíso (see p15) reefs are close inshore, so can be appreciated even by inexperienced divers and snorkelers.

THE SACBÉ OF COBÁ

Cobá was the center of the largest network of *sacbé* (or "white ways"), Mayan raised stone-paved roads, in the Mayan world. They connected the various parts of the city, as well as linked it to vassal-cities. About 800 CE Cobá built the longest ever *sacbé*, of over 60 miles (100 km), to Yaxuná in the west, to help reinforce it in wars with Chichén – unsuccessfully, as Cobá was defeated shortly afterward.

⑨ Sian Ka'an Biosphere Reserve

MAP F5–6

Mexico's largest wetland nature reserve, and a UNESCO World Heritage Site, Sian Ka'an (see pp26–7) brings the Riviera to an end just south of Tulum. Its vast area of virtually untouched mangroves, jungle, and beaches contains an extraordinary range of birds and wildlife, and the one-day tours run by local organizations give a glimpse of the intricate, constantly surprising interplay of nature in this rare environment. The few inhabited spots along the coast are wonderful for fishing, and have a feel of tranquil isolation.

⑩ Xpu-Ha

MAP P5

All along these seven gracefully sweeping bays, 2 miles (3 km) south of Puerto Aventuras, are some of the Riviera's most idyllic beaches, with exuberantly alive reefs and some of the most exquisite turquoise waters. Several are now occupied by resort complexes. However, two (signposted X-4 and X-7 from the highway) are still open to anyone, and at X-7 there are some small cabañas, a camping site, and a dive shop.

COZUMEL IN A DAY

▶ MORNING

Start with breakfast, coffee, or a drink at **Las Palmeras** (see p98), watching the new arrivals off the Playa del Carmen ferry. Browse in the jewelry and souvenir shops along the waterfront and in the streets around the square, but don't buy anything yet. Rent a car and head out of town down Avenida Juárez to the Mayan site of **San Gervasio** (see p91). If you hire the services of a guide at the entrance, don't let them hurry you, but take time to notice the birds and vegetation – as much of an attraction as the site. Back at the main road, head left to meet the east coast at windswept **Punta Santa Cecilia** (see p14). Turn south down the road beside the rocks and waves for a lunch of mixed fish and seafood on the beach at **Chen Río** (see p99).

AFTERNOON

Carry on down the coast to **Punta Sur Eco Beach Park** (see p15). From the parking lot, walk down to Punta Celaraín lighthouse and the strange little Mayan temple called the Caracol, and follow the nature trail to try and see some crocodiles and flamingos.

You can snorkel at Punta Sur, but you'll see more marine life if you carry on to **Laguna Chankanaab** (see p14). If all you want is a placid beach, call in at **Playa San Francisco** (see p95). Drive back to town, and don't miss the sunset from the waterfront Malecón. Take another look at the shops, and buy anything you may have spotted on your morning walk.

See map on pp90–91

The Best of the Rest

1 Paamul
MAP Q5

The favorite destination for RV travelers, who take advantage of generous long-term rates to settle in for the whole winter. The campsite also has cabañas (see p129), a beach bar (see p95), and a dive shop.

2 Xel-Ha Site
MAP P6 ■ Open 8:30am–7pm daily ■ Adm

Across the highway from the popular snorkel park, this Mayan city is one of the oldest in the region. On some buildings there are murals dating back to about 200 CE.

3 Aktun-Ha Cenote/ Car Wash
MAP N6

Another fine swimming-hole cenote set amid rocks and woods toward Cobá. Snorkelers can explore the huge main cavern; divers (with guides) can go further.

Visitors inside the Aktun-Ha Cenote

4 Tankah
MAP P6

Off the beaten track, Tankah is a placid, narrow beach with a fine reef, a restaurant, and a small cluster of villas and hotels. Behind the beach,

by the Casa Cenote restaurant, there's a broad, reed-lined cenote, so it's a toss-up between swimming in the surf or the freshwater pool.

5 Dos Ojos Cenote
MAP P6

Dos Ojos (see p58) is very possibly the world's longest underwater cave system. The snorkeling or diving tours run by the diving tour operators are a memorable experience.

6 Gran Cenote
MAP N6

The Cobá road north from Tulum is one of the best places to find swimmable cenotes, and this (see p59) is one of the most beautiful – crystal-clear pool that's a must-try for swimmers and snorkelers.

7 Muyil Site
MAP G4 ■ Open 8am–5pm daily ■ Adm

The location is the attraction of this old, atmospheric Mayan city set in hot, steamy jungle between the Highway and Lake Chunyaxché, in the Sian Ka'an reserve.

8 Aktun-Chen Cave
MAP P5

This giant cave (see p57) in thick jungle in a nature park has a series of chambers and stalagmite towers, plus an underground river.

9 Punta Laguna
MAP N4

Set in a tiny village by a forest lake north of Cobá, this nature reserve (see p56) is one of the best places to see spider monkeys in the Yucatán. Villagers will act as guides.

10 Road from Boca Paila to Punta Allen
MAP G4–5

Good for the adventurous, this is one of the bumpiest, rutted, overgrown, and deserted roads in the Yucatán, with great vistas of sea and forest.

➤ *See map on pp90–91*

Beaches

Enjoying the waters at Playa Sol

① Playa San Francisco and Playa Sol, Cozumel
MAP R5–6

These are two of the many great beaches on Cozumel's southwest coast: San Francisco and others near it are good for relaxation; Sol is best if you want a beach with lots going on.

② South Beach, Tulum
MAP P6

The place for people who want to find some seclusion in Tulum, with longer, broader, whiter beaches, acres of space, and quite luxurious comforts in some cabañas.

③ Media Luna Bay, Akumal
MAP P5

"Half Moon Bay" is an exquisite crescent of brilliant white sand and calm sea. The atmosphere is just as tranquil: around it there are condos and villas; at the north end is the lovely Yal-Ku (see p65) lagoon.

④ Paamul
MAP Q5

A curving white-sand bay (see p129) with a beach bar and cabañas. With over a mile (2 km) of beach, the campsite doesn't obstruct the view, and the sands are never crowded.

⑤ Xpu-Ha
MAP P5

Seven bays (see p93) with some of the coolest, whitest sand and most colorful coral on the Riviera. Several are occupied by resorts, but X-4 and X-7 are open to anyone.

⑥ Chen Río, Cozumel
MAP R5

This is the best beach on Cozumel's rugged eastern shore, with a sheltered cove for swimming, with surfing further along. There's a beach restaurant worth a special visit.

⑦ Akumal Village
MAP P5

A bustling beach in the center of Akumal; behind it there's a good choice of low-key bars and shops.

⑧ North Beach, Tulum
MAP P6

The beaches at the north end of Tulum (see pp22–3) are great if you want to hang out and meet people in the inexpensive cabañas. They also have the best view of the Mayan site.

⑨ Punta Xamach and Conoco
MAP G5

Getting to these remote, deserted beaches involves negotiating the wild, rutted road between Boca Paila and Punta Allen.

⑩ Punta Solimán
MAP P6

Shaded by palms, this near-empty beach feels remote, even though it's only down a dirt-track from the highway. A few boats and a bar (see p98) are the main signs of habitation.

Tranquil Punta Solimán

Places to Shop

1 Azul Gallery, Cozumel
MAP R5 ■ 449 Av 15 Norte, between Calle 8 and Calle 10

Watch artist Greg Dietrich engrave blown glass to create unique vessels and lamps at this quaint art gallery. Paintings, jewelry, and other items made by local artists are also on display.

Engraved glass, Azul Gallery

2 Punta Langosta, Cozumel
MAP R5

This leisure mall set in the cruise terminal has major international fashion names plus upscale handicrafts and glittering gem stores.

3 Josa, Tulum
MAP P6 ■ (984) 115 8441 ■ Carretera Boca Paila, km 1.5 Quintana Roo, Tulum

Inspired by the tropical and relaxed vibe of the Tulum beaches, this chic boutique sells fashionable accessories and clothing for women.

4 Tulum Bazaar, Tulum
MAP P6 ■ Av Tulum

An amazing hotchpotch of stores in true Mexican flea-market style. Souvenirs, Mayan handicrafts, textiles, and jewelry abound. Be ready to haggle for the best deals.

5 Los Cinco Soles, Cozumel
MAP R5 ■ Av Rafael Melgar 27, by Calle 8

This Malecón handicrafts store is the place to do all your souvenir shopping in one go – clothes, tablecloths, jewelry, glassware, metal or papier-mâché birds and animals, and more.

6 Unicornio, Cozumel
MAP R5 ■ Av 5 Sur, near Calle 1 Sur

A big, varied crafts dealer, with especially good ceramics and painted wood. There's junk as well as quality pieces, but it's a great place to browse.

7 Shalom, Tulum
MAP P6 ■ Av Tulum, between Calle Orion and Calle Centauro

Get dressed for a Tulum-style beach party at this cool shop selling hippy-style clothing plus sleeker items that you could wear when out clubbing.

8 Pro Dive, Cozumel
MAP R5 ■ Av Adolfo Rosado Salas 198, corner of Av 5

First port of call for self-sufficient sea-explorers, with every possible kind of diving and snorkeling gear.

9 Puerto Aventuras
MAP Q5

A small, stylish group of shops. Among the cigars and sophisticated jewelry, you'll also find Mexican designer clothing at Arte Maya and fine handicrafts at El Guerrero.

10 Mixik Artesanías, Tulum
MAP P6 ■ Av Tulum, opposite the bus terminal

This little store has a high-quality collection of colorful craftwork from every part of the country.

A toy shop on the sidewalk, Tulum

Nightspots

1 Al Cielo, Puerto Aventuras

MAP Q5 ▪ Xpu-Ha Beach ▪ Open 11:30am–9pm daily ▪ Adm

The exclusive Al Cielo offers guests one-of-a-kind events on Xpu-Ha Beach, often with the moonlit ocean as a backdrop. It features top-class musicians, dancers, and other entertainment.

2 La Internacional Cervecería, Cozumel

MAP R5 ▪ (987) 869 1289 ▪ Av Rafael Melgar, by 7 Sur and 11 Sur

With a focus on beers, this bar offers a fine selection of international and Mexican brews, specially sourced from craft brewers around the country.

3 Plaza del Sol, Cozumel

MAP R5 ▪ Av Melgar at Av Juárez

Cozumel doesn't have a particularly wild nightlife. Instead, San Miguel's central plaza is the best place to be – especially on Sundays, when there's usually live music.

4 La Zebra, Tulum

MAP G4 ▪ Beach Rd, km 4.6

La Zebra's Sunday night salsa party draws people from up and down the beach as well as from town. Come early for free dance classes.

5 Hard Rock Café, Cozumel

MAP R5 ▪ Av Rafael Melgar 2A ▪ Open from 10pm daily ▪ Adm

The Mayan-style architecture of the building makes this a stunning location for the rock memorabilia chain. Occasional live music.

6 Jimmy Buffett's Margaritaville, Cozumel

MAP R5 ▪ Av Rafael Melgar 799, Col Centro ▪ Open 9am–11pm Mon–Sat

On the water, with great views and familiar fare, this branch of the chain is a huge hit with visitors.

7 Joel's Bar, Puerto Aventuras

MAP Q5 ▪ On the Marina ▪ Open 4pm–1am daily

Enjoy a wide range of entertainment, such as live music performances, preceded or accompanied by dinner at this amazing bar.

Carlos'n Charlie's, Cozumel

8 Carlos'n Charlie's, Cozumel

MAP R5 ▪ Av Rafael Melgar 551 ▪ Open from 11am daily

Cozumel's biggest bar, restaurant, and music venue (see p67) is the place where you're assured of finding a (usually pretty raucous) crowd every night, partying in the open air to classic rock circa 1970 to present.

9 Kin Toh, Tulum

MAP P6 ▪ Carretera Tulum-Punta Allen km 5

Treetop hangouts called "nests" overlooking the jungle are a famous feature of Kin Toh (see p66). Cocktails have local spirits and ingredients, such as *xtabentún*, a Yucatecan liqueur made with honey and notes of anise.

10 Mezzanine, Tulum

MAP P6 ▪ Carretera Boca Paila, km 1.5 ▪ Open from 11am daily ▪ No credit cards ▪ Adm

This stylish restaurant-bar combines luxurious indulgence with eco-friendly policies. Enjoy one of their cocktails while chilling to the sounds of guest DJs.

See map on pp90–91

Drinking and Entertainment Spots

1 Teetotum
MAP P6 ■ $$

On the road between Tulum town and the beach, Teetotum is attached to the hotel of the same name. The cocktail list – try the "Mayan Elder": mezcal, angostura bitters, orange, and cherry juice – and laid-back vibe make it a cool spot for an evening drink.

Colorful exterior of Las Palmeras

2 Las Palmeras, Cozumel
MAP R5 ■ Av Rafael Melgar–Plaza Cozumel ■ $$

A big and friendly Caribbean hut of a bar, Las Palmeras is set opposite the ferry landing on San Miguel's main plaza. It is great for drinks, and it does highly enjoyable breakfasts.

3 Casa Mission Restaurant
MAP R5 ■ Av Lic. Benito Juárez 55 ■ $$

Housed in an old mission, this place specializes in Mexican classics, such as Veracruz-style fish, featuring a tomato sauce dotted with olives.

4 Viva México, Cozumel
MAP R5 ■ Av Rafael E. Melgar ■ $

This is one of the few cafés with a sea view in San Miguel, serving margaritas, mojitos, and daiquiris, and classic Mexican and American food.

5 Café del Museo, Cozumel
MAP R5 ■ Av Rafael Melgar, by Calle 4 ■ Open 9am–5pm daily ■ $

This very relaxing, pretty café on the roof of Cozumel's museum (see p14) has a great view of the waterfront and good coffee. It does tasty breakfasts and snacks too.

6 Mezcalito's, Cozumel
MAP R5 ■ Punta Santa Cecilia ■ $$

An old favorite, this relaxed beach restaurant is set in a wonderful location, where the cross-island road meets the east coast. Enjoy a soundtrack of crashing surf.

7 Cabañas Paamul
MAP Q5 ■ $

Deep shade and an ideal view over the beach make the bar in the Paamul cabañas and camping site (see p129) a great place to recharge after time in the sun. Snacks are also available.

8 Piña Colada, Puerto Aventuras
MAP Q5 ■ $

Puerto Aventuras' favorite beach bar has a big palapa roof. Elaborate tropical cocktails are the specialty.

9 Oscar y Lalo, Punta Solimán
MAP P6 ■ $

Punta Solimán has a desert-island feel, and so does its only bar. Oscar and Lalo, who also run the camping site and rent kayaks, are friendly and cook great fresh seafood.

10 El Paraíso, Tulum
MAP P6 ■ Beach Rd, km 5.5 ■ $

Many of Tulum's cabaña-clusters have bars, but Paraíso, near the ruins, has the best view, with a big terrace for catching the breeze.

Places to Eat

PRICE CATEGORIES
For a three-course meal for one with a beer or soda (or equivalent meal), taxes, and extra charges.

$ under $15 $$ $15–$35 $$$ over $35

1 Guido's, Cozumel
MAP R5 ■ Av Melgar 23, between Calle 6 and Calle 8 ■ (987) 872 0946 ■ $$$

Known for its rich lasagne, Guido's serves great Italian food. Enjoy your food outside in the garden.

2 Rock'n Java, Cozumel
MAP R5 ■ Av Rafael Melgar 602, between Calle 7 and Av Quintana Roo ■ (987) 872 4405 ■ $$

The big fresh salads and sandwiches are great at this American-run café on the water. Save some room for a huge slice of apple pie or one of the other gooey desserts.

Seating area, Casa Denis

3 Casa Denis, Cozumel
MAP R5 ■ Calle 1 Sur ■ From 7am daily ■ No credit cards ■ $$

One of the island's oldest venues, Casa Denis serves classic Yucatecan dishes (see pp68–9) at low prices.

4 Arca
MAP P6 ■ Av Tulum-Boca Paila, km 7.6 ■ (984) 112 6823 ■ Closed L & Mon ■ $$$

"From fire to table" is the motto of this restaurant, where the menu changes regularly. Seasonal and locally-sourced produce is prepared by a chef who has worked in the world's top restaurants.

5 La Cocay, Cozumel
MAP R5 ■ Calle 8, between Av 10 and Av 15 ■ $$$

Set in a Caribbean-style wooden hut, this mellow place offers a range of Mediterranean-inspired dishes.

6 La Palapa de Marlon
MAP Q5 ■ Calzada Puerto Maya, Lote 5 ■ Open 9am–5pm Mon, noon–7:30pm Tue–Sun ■ $

Try some of the region's best seafood here. Dishes include shrimp, fish, and octopus tacos, and nine different types of ceviche.

7 Tequilaville, Akumal
MAP P5 ■ Calle Principal ■ (984) 875 9022 ■ $$

This small restaurant serves a pleasant selection of traditional Mexican food and, allegedly, the best hamburger in the Riviera Maya.

8 Cetli, Tulum
MAP P6 ■ Calle Polar at Calle Orion ■ (984) 108 0681 ■ $$

A Mexico City-trained chef-owner turns out light, refined versions of Mexican classics such as *chiles en nogada* (stuffed chilies with walnut sauce) at this casual spot.

9 Hartwood, Tulum
MAP P6 ■ Tulum Beach Rd, km 7.6 ■ $$$

Across from the beach and set in lush jungle, Hartwood's chefs cook over an open fire and produce top-class cuisine. Reservations are strongly suggested.

10 Chen Río, Cozumel
MAP R5 ■ Chen Río Beach ■ No credit cards ■ $$

The best restaurant on Cozumel's east coast, and a wonderful place to eat on the beach.

See map on pp90–91

The Central Heartland

TOP 10

An unmistakable Yucatecan identity and sense of culture distinguishes towns such as Valladolid or Tizimín, with Spanish-era churches and squares, Mayan women selling delicious fruit and colorful flowers, and a gently paced street life. The ancestors of the modern Maya built some of their greatest creations here, at Ek-Balam and

Brown pelican

the city of Chichén Itzá. Giant underground caverns and magical cenote pools lie beneath the landscape.

1 Balankanché Caves

MAP E3 ▪ Open 8am–5pm daily ▪ Adm

This great labyrinthine complex of caves extends for miles under the Yucatán forest. Caves were sacred for the ancient Maya and, in one spectacular chamber, the sanctuary, remains were found of over 100 ritual incense burners. The compulsory tour ends in a magical chamber with a perfectly still pool, in which the cave bottom seen through the water is a mirror image of the roof.

THE CENTRAL HEARTLAND

Map legend:
- **1** Top 10 Sights *see pp100–103*
- **1** Places to Eat *see p107*
- **1** Shops, Markets, and Tours *see p105*
- **1** The Best of the Rest *see p104*
- **1** Drinking and Entertainment Spots *see p106*

Map locations include: Gulf of Mexico, Río Lagartos, San Felipe, Parque Nacional San Felipe, Loche, Panaba, Yalsihon, Dzilam de Bravo, Telchac and Uaymitún, Santa Clara, Dzidzantun, Dzilam González, La Gran Lucha, Sucila, Kikil, Tizimín, Dzemul, Telchac, Cansahcab, Temax, Buctzotz, Santo Domingo, Tixbacab, Calotm, Motul, Tixkokob, Tekanto, Tekal de Venégas, Cenotillo, Espita, Aké, Izamal, Xuilub, Ek-Balam, Tahmek, Tunkas, Dzitas, Temozón, Tinúm, Yokdzonot, Pisté, Chichén Itzá, Balankanché Caves, See Valladolid map, right, Yaxcabá, Chankom, Dzitnup and Samula Cenote, Tixcalpupul, Tixcacltuyub, Xcopteil, Xuxcab

15 miles (24 km)

2 San Felipe
MAP E1

To the west of Río Lagartos (see p57), this village (see p62) is smaller and has a superb, usually near-empty beach on the sandbar across the lagoon, facing the opal waters of the Gulf of Mexico. Village boatmen will ferry you to and from the beach, and also offer flamingo tours. You can see fabulous sunsets from the village.

3 Dzitnup and Samula Cenote
MAP E3 ▪ Dzitnup village ▪ Open 8am–5pm daily ▪ Adm

Easily accessible from Valladolid, these two spectacular swimmable cenotes (see pp58–9) are among some of the greatest sights of the Yucatán. Dzitnup can be entered through a cramped tunnel, which

The huge cavern of Dzitnup Cenote

emerges into a vast, cathedral-like cavern, pierced by a shaft of sunlight and filled with tower-shaped rocks. Only a five-minute walk away, Samula is a large, shallow pool of crystal-clear water, into which the roots of an aged tree dangle through a crack in the rocky ceiling.

Aké's mysterious columns

4 Aké
MAP C2 ▪ Open 8am–5pm daily ▪ Adm ▪ www.inah.gob.mx

This city west of Izamal is a mystery, as its drum-shaped columns and ramp-like stairways are quite unlike other Mayan buildings. The local church was built on an ancient Mayan pyramid (see p45). Alongside the site is a 19th-century *henequén* hacienda, San Lorenzo de Aké, filled with vintage machinery.

Visitor exploring the magnificent Mayan site of Ek-Balam

⑤ Ek-Balam

MAP F2 ■ Open 8am–5pm daily ■ Adm ■ www.inah.gob.mx

In 1998, excavations revealed some of the finest examples of Mayan sculpture here *(see p44)*, on the giant temple-mound known as the Acropolis. Most spectacular is El Trono (The Throne), a temple entrance believed to be the tomb of Ukit-Kan-Lek-Tok, who ruled around 800 CE. Nearby is an intricate mass of finely carved figures. The rest of the Acropolis is a multilevel palace.

⑥ Río Lagartos

MAP F1

This quiet village *(see p63)* on the remote north coast is at the head of over 12 miles (20 km) of mangrove lagoon *(see p57)* and mud flats, with the Yucatán's largest colonies of flamingos and a dazzling variety of other birds. Local boatmen offer good-value tours.

Young eagle, Río Lagartos

⑦ Chichén Itzá

This *(see pp28–31)* is the most famous and awe-inspiring of the great ancient Mayan cities, and the one with the most spine-tingling images of war and sacrifice. The great pyramid of El Castillo, the giant Ball Court, the Sacred Cenote, and the Temple of the Warriors are all must-sees.

⑧ Valladolid

MAP E3 ■ San Bernardino: Parque de San Bernardino; open 9am–8pm Wed–Mon

The Spanish capital of the eastern Yucatán, founded in 1545, has one of the most charming of the region's colonial plazas, overlooked by the tall white cathedral. Valladolid is famed for embroidery, and the square is a good place to buy traditional white, flower-patterned *huipil* blouses and tablecloths. Around town are many fine old Spanish churches and houses, including the beautifully renovated 17th-century townhouse, Casa de los Venados, housing a collection of contemporary Mexican folk art. Four blocks from the plaza you can look down into the pit of Cenote Zací, once Valladolid's main water source. Close by is the San Bernardino de Siena *(see p46)*. Begun in 1552, it *(see p72)* is the oldest permanent church in the Yucatán, with a shady gallery of graceful arches along the facade and a cloister of giant, squat stone columns set around a garden. Inside are some rare 18th-century Baroque altars and altarpieces.

9 **Telchac and Uaymitún**
MAP C/D2

Far west of San Felipe, a road runs along the coast through quiet fishing villages. Seaward, there are endless, often empty, beaches; on the landward side is a lagoon full of birds. Telchac is a fishing harbor with fine beaches and a few cheap hotels and low-key restaurants. At Uaymitún *(see p57)* there is a free observation tower for bird-watching in the lagoon.

10 **Izamal**
MAP D2

The most unaltered Spanish-era city *(see p48)* in the Yucatán, known as *ciudad dorada* or "Golden City" for the color of its buildings, is centered on the huge San Antonio monastery *(see p46)*, begun in 1549 and the shrine of Our Lady of Izamal, the region's patron saint. A short walk away are the remains of three pyramids, traces of a much older Mayan city.

Golden-colored building, Izamal

THE SALT OF CHICHÉN

Salt was one of the greatest sources of wealth in ancient America. In the lagoons near Río Lagartos there are huge salt flats, still exploited today. Around 800 CE, Chichén Itzá won control of them and built its own port at El Cerritos, east of Río Lagartos, to trade in salt. The wealth this gave Chichén was a major reason why it could dominate the Yucatán.

A TWO-DAY TOUR

DAY ONE

Stay the night in **Valladolid**, or the little town of Pisté (close to **Chichén Itzá**), or better still one of the hotels just outside the sites such as **Hacienda Chichén** *(see p126)*. Get to the site as soon as possible to beat the crowds. You'll need at least three hours for exploring the site, before lunch at the charming **Las Mestizas** in Pisté *(see p107)*.

In the afternoon, make a choice: if you're interested in the ancient Maya, go up to **Ek-Balam**, or head into Valladolid for a wander around its plaza, San Bernardino monastery *(see p46)*, and the dramatic town cenote. Before the day ends, head north to **Río Lagartos** *(see p57)* (65 miles/105 km) to reserve a flamingo tour for the next morning. Stay at the **Hotel San Felipe** *(see p131)* in San Felipe.

DAY TWO

The flamingos are best seen early, so you'll be off around 7am. A two- or four-hour tour takes you into an exuberant, rare natural world, through broad lagoons and narrow creeks. Afterward, for lunch, have a *ceviche* at Isla Contoy on the waterfront, or head to Tizimín *(see p104)* for locally sourced seafood at **Casa Makech** *(see p107)* on its colonial square. From Tizimín, turn westward through miles and miles of cattle ranches to reach **Izamal**. Here you can look out on the town from the monastery's arcaded courtyard. The town's golden colors are especially lovely in the warm, early evening light.

See map on pp100–101

The Best of the Rest

1 Ik Kil Cenote
MAP E3 ▪ Highway 180, 2 miles (3 km) E of Chichén Itzá ▪ Open 8am–5pm daily ▪ Adm

A huge, circular pit filled with a beautiful underground pool – now the center of a private nature park. You can swim in the cenote pool and dine in the restaurant up above it.

2 Yaxcabá
MAP D3

This tranquil little town in the woods surprises with its imposing 18th-century church, which features a unique three-tower facade and a beautifully carved wooden altarpiece.

3 Calotmul
MAP F2

Between Valladolid and Tizimín, this is another country town that has a fine church (1749) with a magnificently ornate Baroque altarpiece.

4 Tizimín
MAP F2

The hub of Yucatán's "cattle country" is a non-touristy market town (see p48). At its center are two spacious squares, divided by the massive walls of two Spanish monasteries.

5 Tihosuco
MAP E4 ▪ Museum: open 10am–6pm Tue–Sun ▪ Adm

This remote village 30 miles (48 km) south of Valladolid was where the great Mayan revolt of the Caste War (see p43) began; it still bears the battle scars. A small museum tells visitors the whole story.

6 El Cuyo
MAP F1

At the end of a lonely road through savanna, forest, and sand flats, this tiny fishing village (see p63) is a place to enjoy miles of Gulf coast beaches.

7 Bocas de Dzilam
MAP D1

This vast area of mangroves west of San Felipe is remote and wild. There are no regular tours, but boatmen in San Felipe or Dzilam may offer a trip.

8 El Bajo and Santa Clara
MAP D1

Alongside the north coast road is a long, narrow sand-spit island, El Bajo, with deserted, coconut-palm shaded beaches. In the tiny village of Santa Clara you can find boatmen offering trips to the island.

9 Xcambó
MAP C2 ▪ (999) 913 4034 ▪ Open 8am–5pm daily ▪ Adm

The atmospheric site of a coastal Mayan town, probably an outlying Dzibilchaltún settlement, with great views from the top of its pyramid.

10 Cenote Yokdzonot
MAP E3 ▪ Yokdzonot village, 9 miles (14 km) west of Pisté ▪ Open 9am–6pm daily ▪ Adm

The little-visited village of Yokdzonot, a short drive from Pisté and Chichén Itzá, is home to a delightful, vine-clad cenote, perfect for an afternoon dip. Life jackets and snorkeling gear are available.

Fortified church, Tihosuco

Shops, Markets, and Tours

1 Main Plaza, Valladolid
MAP E3

Mayan women from the surrounding villages display their beautifully bright *huípiles* (traditional blouses) and other embroidery on the railings of the Parque Principal.

2 MexiGo Tours, Valladolid
MAP E3 ▪ Calle 43, by Calle 40 and Calle 42 ▪ (985) 856 0777 ▪ www.mexigotours.com

Owned and managed by locals, this outfitter offers guided tours for archaeological and historical sites in and around Valladolid. Bike rental is also available.

3 Handicrafts Market, Chichén Itzá
MAP E3

Around the Chichén Itzá visitor center there is something approaching a mall of handicrafts stalls, some of which are run by Maya selling their own embroidery, woven hammocks, and wood carvings.

4 Flamingo Tours, Río Lagartos
MAP F1 ▪ (986) 862 0542

The best local boatmen's cooperative has a kiosk on the waterfront *(see p57)*, just left of where the Tizimín road runs out. They work alongside the nature reserve and have good boats and experienced guides.

5 San Felipe Tours
MAP E1 ▪ (986) 100 8390

The boatmen's cooperative here is a bit less organized but also has a waterfront hut, in San Felipe village. Rates are similar to those in Río Lagartos, but boatmen here will be more ready to take you to the Bocas de Dzilam *(see p104)* and Río Lagartos lagoon *(see p57)*.

Handicrafts at Valladolid Market

Chichén Itzá

6 Valladolid Crafts Market and Bazaar
MAP E3 ▪ Mercado de Artesanías Calle 39, corner of Calle 44

Valladolid's semi-official handicrafts market has some fine embroidery, as well as more mass-produced goods. The nearby bazaar is a quirky set of shops around a food court *(see p107)*.

7 Market, Tizimín
MAP F2 ▪ Open 8am–5pm daily

Not a place for souvenirs but a real, bustling country town market, with great fruit and produce and household goods.

8 Yalat, Valladolid
MAP E3 ▪ Corner of Calle 39 and Calle 40

Set on Valladolid's central plaza, Yalat offers jewelry, embroidered clothes, Mexican chocolate, and sisal-fiber bath scrubs.

9 Hecho a Mano, Izamal
MAP D2 ▪ Calle 31, No. 308, by the Town Hall

A pretty little shop with a more carefully selected display of hand-made folk art than in the markets, as well as striking photographs of Yucatecan scenes.

10 Market, Izamal
MAP D2 ▪ Calle 31/Calle 32

Izamal's market, just below the monastery, has a mix of souvenirs, handicrafts, and busy little cafés.

See map on pp100–101

Drinking and Entertainment Spots

1 Absenta Pub, Valladolid
MAP E3 ■ Parque Flamboyanes
■ (985) 856 0763 ■ Open 6pm–2am
daily ■ $

This popular watering hole is known for chicken wings, burgers, and fried mozzarella sticks, as well as its live music and attentive servers.

2 Restaurante Zaci, Valladolid
MAP E3 ■ Calle 37 ■ (985) 856 0721 ■ $

Generous portions of local specialities are served here under a palapa, all in sight of the Zaci cenote. You can even take a dip before or after your meal.

3 Hacienda Chichén
MAP E3 ■ Hotel Zone, Chichén Itzá ■ $$$

This historic ranch-hotel, on the fringes of the Chichén Itzá site, has a terrace restaurant-bar perfect for a cocktail after a day of exploration.

Guests at Hacienda Chichén

4 Hotel María de la Luz, Valladolid
MAP E3 ■ Calle 42 ■ $$

This hotel has a big, well-shaded terrace on the Parque Principal, with very comfortable seats – ideal for lazy lounging while keeping an eye on all the movement in the square.

5 Soletana Café Santuario, Valladolid
MAP E3 ■ Calzada de Los Frailes 209
■ (985) 130 0069 ■ Open 8am–10:30pm
daily ■ $

Located inside the Verde Morada hotel, this café serves pour-over coffee and drinks inspired by local ingredients.

6 Pueblo Maya, Pisté
MAP E3 ■ Calle 15, No. 48B, Manzana No. 13 ■ $

Enjoy tasty Mexican food at Pueblo Maya, which is also a craft market. It has a lovely pool and hammocks to lounge in after your meal.

7 Anahata Café and Bistro, El Cuyo
MAP F1 ■ Av Veraniega, Calle 17, No. 142 ■ Open 7:30am–1pm daily ■ $

This café serves a variety of coffee, including an unusual pink latte. Try its other offbeat items like avocado toast with *chapulines* (grasshoppers).

8 Ria Maya, Río Lagartos
MAP F1 ■ (986) 862 0045 ■ Calle 19, by Calle 13 and Calle 14 ■ $$

Popular for its seafood, the menu at this family-friendly restaurant is complemented not only by its settings but also fine sunset views.

9 Market Bars, Izamal
MAP D2 ■ Calle 31, by Calle 32 ■ $

Several cafés and *loncherías* here share an outside terrace, a fine vantage point on the monastery and town life. Some serve beer; some only soft drinks with their snacks.

10 Sunday Concerts, Valladolid
MAP E3 ■ Parque Principal
■ Open from 7:30pm Sun

Valladolid puts on entertainment for free – the town band gives a concert every Sunday night in the square, with a wide-ranging musical menu.

Places to Eat

PRICE CATEGORIES

For a three-course meal for one with a beer of soda (or equivalent meal), taxes and extra charges.

$ under $15 **$$** $15–$35 **$$$** over $35

① Restaurante El Toro, Izamal

MAP D2 ▪ Plazuela 2 de Abril ▪ (998) 954 1169 ▪ No credit cards ▪ $

Set on a square near the monastery is this friendly little restaurant, with tasty Yucatecan dishes and tacos.

② Cocinas Económicas, Valladolid

MAP E3 ▪ Calle 39, on Parque Principal ▪ No credit cards ▪ $

Around the bazaar on the square (see p105) there's a line of self-service food counters. Noisy, with lots of atmosphere, this is a great place for a good breakfast, and to try out local snacks.

③ Casa Italia, Valladolid

MAP E3 ▪ Calle 35, No. 202 ▪ $

Overlooking a quaint plaza a short walk from the city center, this family-run restaurant serves the best Italian food in Valladolid, drawing a loyal crowd of locals and visitors. The thin-crust pizzas and pasta dishes are delicious and good value.

④ Chaya's Natural Café, Ek-Balam

MAP F2 ▪ Off the NE Cnr of the town plaza ▪ $$

The restaurant at Genesis Retreat (see p129) is open to non-guests only in the afternoon, but the crêpes and chocolate-chili cookies make it well worth a visit.

⑤ Las Mestizas, Pisté

MAP E3 ▪ (985) 851 0069 ▪ No credit cards ▪ $$

The prettiest of the restaurants along the main road in Pisté, with charming service. It dishes up a delicious sopa de lima (see p69).

⑥ Hostería del Marqués, Valladolid

MAP E3 ▪ Calle 39, on Parque Principal ▪ (985) 856 3042 ▪ $$

Valladolid's best hotel also has its most eminent restaurant, with tables around a plant-filled patio. Its versions of local specialties like lomitos de Valladolid are definitive.

Patio dining at Hostería del Marqués

⑦ Casa Makech, Tizimín

MAP F2 ▪ Calle 51, No. 403 ▪ (986) 113 7131 ▪ $

This spot uses fresh, local ingredients to create dishes like octopus marinated in achiote, bitter orange, and sweet chili. Ask for a seat in the shady garden.

⑧ Yerba Buena del Sisal, Valladolid

MAP E3 ▪ Calle 54A No. 217 ▪ (985) 856 1406 ▪ $

This charming restaurant is decorated with papel picado banners and is a great option for vegetarians.

⑨ Restaurante Vaselina, San Felipe

MAP E1 ▪ (986) 862 2083 ▪ $$

A big, unfussy place on the seafront where you can try wonderfully fresh, fat shrimp, octopus, and conch.

⑩ Kinich, Izamal

MAP D2 ▪ Calle 27, No. 299, between Calle 28 and Calle 30 ▪ (988) 954 0489 ▪ Closed D ▪ $$

Set in a lush garden, this place has a high reputation for classic Yucatecan food, such as poc-chuc (see p68).

See map on pp100–101

TOP 10 The West

Arch of Labná

Nowhere is the flavor of the Yucatán more intense than in the west of the region, around its historic capital, Mérida. In these parts, there is an extraordinary density of Mayan relics and, although they may not match the awe-inspiring power of Chichén Itzá, sites such as Uxmal show the architecture of the Maya at its most elegant. Beyond the main sights are stretches of wilderness, hidden lagoons, and small towns dripping with bougainvillea and hibiscus.

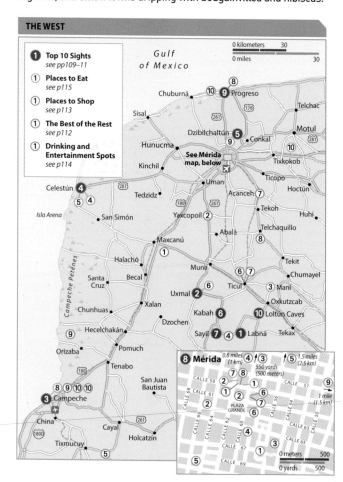

THE WEST

1 **Top 10 Sights**
see pp109–11

1 **Places to Eat**
see p115

1 **Places to Shop**
see p113

1 **The Best of the Rest**
see p112

1 **Drinking and Entertainment Spots**
see p114

Gulf of Mexico

Chuburná · Progreso
Sisal · Telchac
Dzibilchaltún · Conkal · Motul
Hunucma · Tixkokob
Kinchil · Ticopo
Umán · Hoctún
Celestún · Acanceh · Tekoh
Tedzidz · Tekit
Isla Arena · San Simón · Yaxcopoil · Abalá · Telchaquillo
Maxcanú · Huhi
Halachó · Muna · Tekit
Santa Cruz · Becal · Ticul · Chumayel
Chunhuas · Xalan · Uxmal · Maní
Hecelchakán · Kabah · Oxkutzcab · Loltún Caves
Orizaba · Dzochen · Sayil · Labná · Tekax
Pomuch
Tenabo
San Juan Bautista
Campeche
China
Cayal · Holcatzin
Tixmucuy

Mérida

PLAZA GRANDE

1 Labná
MAP C4 ■ Open 8am–5pm daily ■ Adm

The Arch of Labná, wonderfully drawn by Frederick Catherwood *(see p110)*, exemplifies the sophistication of Puuc architecture. Nearby, the town's Palacio is only slightly smaller than Sayil's, and was divided into seven patios – the part to the left (west) was home to the lords of Labná, while the patios to the right were for servants. The setting, in tranquil woods full of birds, is especially lovely.

2 Uxmal
With the elegant lines of the Nunnery Quadrangle and towering mass of the Pyramid of the Magician, Uxmal *(see pp34–5)* is not only one of the most beautiful of ancient Mayan cities but also one of the greatest sights in the Americas.

3 Campeche
This Spanish-era walled city *(see pp38–9)* retains a charming old-world feel. The 17th-century ramparts and bastions were built to defend it against pirates. The streets within are lined with delicately colored old houses featuring patios and iron-grilled windows. A museum, housed in an old Spanish fort, contains jade funeral masks and other fine relics from the excavated site at Calakmul.

Colorful colonial Campeche

Flamingos at Celestún

4 Celestún
MAP A3 ■ Tours from Celestún Embarcadero: 8am–5pm daily ■ Adm

Just north of this fishing village is a silent, watery expanse of mangrove lagoon that is a breeding ground for flamingos, ibises, egrets, and blue herons. Boat tours are very popular (the lagoon can get rather crowded at times). Stay over in Celestún after the tours have gone back to Mérida to enjoy this tranquil village, with its white beach, laid-back restaurants and hotels, and fabulous sunsets.

STEPHENS AND CATHERWOOD

The existence of an ancient Mayan civilization was brought to the world's attention by the American traveler John Lloyd Stephens (1805–52) and English artist Frederick Catherwood (1799–1854). Traveling together from 1839 to 1842, they provided the first full descriptions and drawings of Chichén Itzá and Uxmal, and are credited with the rediscovery of Kabah and Sayil, among others.

Cenote Xlacah, Dzibilchaltún

5 Dzibilchaltún
MAP C2 ▪ Cenote Xlacah: open 8am–5pm daily ▪ Adm Mon–Fri

The Temple of the Seven Dolls, through which the sun strikes at dawn on spring and fall equinoxes to run straight along a white *sacbé* (rough cast road) to the central plaza, is the most celebrated feature of this Mayan city just north of Mérida. It was one of the longest-inhabited Mayan cities, occupied for over 2,000 years. There are additional temples at the site, as well as a grand Palacio and a Spanish missionary chapel. The huge, mysterious pool – Cenote Xlacah – which provided the ancient city with water, now offers an idyllic place in which to cool off.

6 Kabah
MAP C4 ▪ Open 8am–5pm daily ▪ Adm

This was the second most important of the Puuc cities *(see p37)* after Uxmal, and an imposing arch on its west side marks the start of the *sacbé* road *(see p93)* that linked it to its larger ally. Its Codz Poop, or "Palace of Masks," is the most extravagant example of Mayan carving: the extraordinary facade is covered with 250 faces of the long-nosed rain-god Chac. The Palacio and Temple of the Columns are two more classics of refined Puuc architecture.

7 Sayil
MAP C4 ▪ Open 8am–5pm daily ▪ Adm

Of all the Puuc cities, Sayil is the one that gives the strongest sense of the huge wealth of its ancient inhabitants. Its hub is the magnificent Palacio, an opulent complex that sweeps up through three levels and more than 90 chambers, with an architectural refinement that recalls the buildings of ancient Greece. It housed over 350 people, from lords to servants, and had its own exclusive water supply.

8 Mérida
This *(see pp32–3)* is perhaps the most appealing of all the colonial cities in Mexico, with elegant

Sunday fiesta in Mérida

architecture, shady patios, great markets, and a distinct friendliness. With the soft music of *boleros* and the *jarana* heard in free concerts in 16th-century squares, and fiestas enjoyed by all ages every Sunday, the town's appeal is plentiful and varied.

Progreso's dramatic pier

⑨ Progreso

Mérida's port and favorite beach town is a place to get close to ordinary Yucatecan life. The harbor is set at the end of a 4-mile (6-km) pier, and so the shallow waters around the beach remain blissfully tranquil. It's calm until the weekend, that is, when Meridanos spill out onto the sand and into the warm blue waters. There are excellent fish restaurants along the seafront, too, with large, convivial outside terraces on which to socialize.

⑩ Loltún Caves

MAP C4 ■ Tours 9:30am–4pm daily ■ Adm

This vast cave complex (see p59) is both a stunning natural phenomenon and an ancient Mayan site. It has been occupied by humans longer than anywhere else in the Yucatán, from remote prehistory right up until the 19th century. The ancient Maya lived here, mined the caves, and used them for rituals. Guided tours take you through 1.5 miles (2 km) of caves, but the network extends much further. The rock formations are awe-inspiring, and a special feature of Loltún is its strange changes of temperature, from fierce heat to chilly breezes.

A DAY IN THE PUUC HILLS

▶ MORNING

Leave **Mérida** early in a rental car and drive directly to **Uxmal** (see pp34–5). Beyond the suburb of Umán, where you turn onto Highway 261, traffic thins out, and you'll have an easy drive through woods and a few tranquil villages.

Beyond Muna the road enters the Puuc Hills before descending to Uxmal. Spend at least two hours exploring this site, keeping an eye out for the many iguanas as well as admiring the architecture.

Recoup your energies by heading back up the road to the nearby Hacienda Uxmal (see p115) for *sopa de lima* on the terrace.

AFTERNOON

Head straight for **Kabah** to marvel at the monsters of the Codz Poop.

Further south, the "Puuc Route" turns off the main Highway 261 onto a lovely woodland road, with only a few other tourists, tricycle carts, and the birds for company. Along the way are stop-offs at the Puuc sites of **Sayil, Xlapak** (see p45), and **Labná** (see p109). At the end of the road, descend into the netherworld of the **Loltún Caves**, refreshing yourself afterwards in the café.

Go down to Oxkutzcab, and turn left for **Ticul** (see p112), where you can take a leisurely stroll around its historic Plaza Mayor. Drive back to Mérida, stopping en route at **Yaxcopoíl** (see p112) for a quick tour of the hacienda.

See map on p108 ←

The Best of the Rest

1 Oxkintok
MAP B3 ■ Open 8:30am–5pm daily ■ Adm ■ www.inah.gob.mx

This ancient Mayan city has a Satunsat, or "Labyrinth" pyramid, containing a strange, dark maze, possibly built as an entrance to the Underworld that only the Lord of Oxkintok could use.

2 Yaxcopoíl Hacienda
MAP C3 ■ Open 8am–6pm Mon–Sat, 9am–1pm Sun ■ Adm ■ www.yaxcopoil.com

Of all the restored haciendas in the Yucatán, this one, with its crumbling, ornate main house and factory buildings, gives the best feel of life here when *henequén* or "green gold" (see p43) dominated the state.

3 Cenotes
The cenotes and underwater rivers in the western Yucatán are far less well explored than those around Tulum (see pp22–3). Snorkeling and diving trips are run from Mérida.

4 Xlapak
MAP C4 ■ Open 8am–5pm daily ■ Adm ■ www.inah.gob.mx

The smallest Puuc site (see p37) is as attractive for the undisturbed wood-land walk as for its archaeological site. The Palacio has intricate Puuc carving.

5 Edzná
MAP B5 ■ Open 8am–5pm daily (last entry at 4:30pm) ■ Adm ■ www.inah.gob.mx

This (see p39) is a Mayan city as spectacular as Chichén Itzá. The "Building of the Five Stories" is one of the largest Mayan palaces.

Ochre-colored church in Ticul

6 Ticul
MAP C4

One of the most charming Yucatán country towns (see p49), Ticul is also a historic center for ceramics.

7 Acanceh
MAP C3

On one side of the square of this remarkable little town (see p49) is an 18th-century church, while on another is a very ancient Mayan pyramid, perhaps begun around 300 BCE.

8 Mayapán
MAP C3 ■ Open 8:30am–5pm daily ■ Adm ■ www.inah.gob.mx

The last big Mayan city, and one that dominated the Yucatán for 200 years after 1200. Its buildings often "mimic" Chichén Itzá and have beautifully preserved frescoes.

9 The Campeche Petenés
MAP A4

This mangrove and forest wilderness (see p56) is home to a wide range of wildlife such as pumas and turtles. Trips can be taken from Campeche or the village of Isla Arena.

10 Chelem and Yucalpetén
MAP C2

Just west of Progreso, on the other side of a gap in the coastal sand bar, these easy-going villages have long, almost empty beaches. They're popular for windsurfing.

The site of Edzná

Places to Shop

1 Bazar de Artesanías Craft Market, Mérida
MAP C2 ▪ Calle 67, by corner of Calle 56

This semi-official handicrafts market is packed with stalls selling every kind of Yucatecan and some excellent Mexican craftwork.

2 Casa de Artesanías, Mérida
MAP C2 ▪ Calle 63, No. 503, between Calle 64 and Calle 66

The Yucatán state handicrafts store has high-quality local work, with many beautiful, usable things especially in textiles, basketware, and wood.

3 Mérida Market
MAP C2 ▪ Calle 65, between Calle 54 and Calle 58

One of the world's greatest markets, this is a labyrinth of alleys and stalls selling everything imaginable – fish, fruit, a huge range of chilies, *huipil* blouses, sandals, and hats.

4 Hamacas La Poblana, Mérida
MAP C2 ▪ Calle 65, No. 492, Centro

Street stalls sell low-quality but cheap hammocks – head here for the real thing in every color, size, and style, sold by weight.

5 El Charro Mexicano, Mérida
MAP C2 ▪ 59 515, Zona Paseo Montejo, La Quinta

A little shop selling *botas* (boots) and *sombreros* (hats) opposite the market, with a friendly owner who will show you piles of handmade panamas in all sorts of styles and sizes.

Mérida market pottery

6 Mexicanísimo, Mérida
MAP C2 ▪ Parque Hidalgo Calle 60, between Calle 59 and Calle 61

This is an innovative store that sells lightweight clothes for men and women in original, modern designs, using Mexican cottons and other traditional materials.

7 Arte Maya, Ticul
MAP C4 ▪ Calle 23, No. 301

Ticul produces huge quantities of ceramics. This family-run store stands out for the owners' skills and careful use of traditional and even ancient Mayan techniques.

8 Guayaberas Jack, Mérida
MAP C2 ▪ Calle 59, No. 507, between Calle 60 and Calle 62

The *guayabera* shirt-jacket is the smartest thing for gentlemen to wear in tropical Mérida. This long-established shop sells only *guayaberas*, and can make them to measure.

9 Maya Chuy Bordado, Mérida
MAP C2 ▪ Calle 18, No. 80

This charming shop, tucked away from the crowded shopping streets of Mérida, is the outlet of a women's embroidery cooperative. Blouses, rugs, and other items are beautifully and individually made.

10 Casa de Artesanías Tukulná, Campeche
MAP A5 ▪ Calle 10, No. 333, between Calle 59 and Calle 61

Campeche's state handicrafts store has a great choice of ceramics, embroidery, basketwork, and many other top-quality items that are beautifully displayed.

See map on p108

Drinking and Entertainment Spots

1 La Fundación Mezcalería, Mérida
MAP C2 ▪ Calle 59, No. 509, Parque Santa Lucia, Centro ▪ $

This colorful spot specializes in mezcal-based cocktails. There's usually live or DJ-spun music.

2 Dulcería y Sorbetería El Colón, Mérida
MAP C2 ▪ Calle 59, on the plaza ▪ $

Choose from an array of fruit-flavored sorbets and ice creams at this plaza-front parlor. A popular order is a *champola*, scoops of fruit ice served in a tall glass with milk.

3 La Negrita Cantina, Mérida
MAP C2 ▪ Calle 62, No. 415 ▪ (999) 121 0411 ▪ Open noon–10pm daily ▪ $

Experience Havana at this bar, where the decor, drinks, and music all evoke this Caribbean island.

4 Café Crème, Mérida
MAP C2 ▪ Calle 41, corner of Calle 60 Centro ▪ $$

Located in downtown Mérida, two blocks from Paseo Montejo, this café serves a variety of tasty French snacks and refreshing natural fruit juices.

5 Ku'uk, Mérida
MAP C2 ▪ Av Rómulo Rozo No. 488, by Calle 27 and Calle 27A ▪ (999) 944 3377 ▪ $$$

Indulge in the tasting menu at this upscale restaurant or relax with a cocktail at its bar. There is also a fine collection of wine and beer, with many sourced from around Mexico.

6 Jugos California, Mérida
MAP C2 ▪ Calle 58, No. 505 Centro ▪ $

Juice stands are a wonderful local institution, and Jugos California wins the prize as the best in town. You'll find a number of watermelons, pineapples, papayas, and more.

Courtyard bar of Piedra de Agua

7 Piedra de Agua, Mérida
MAP C2 ▪ Calle 62, No. 498 ▪ $$

In a boutique hotel of the same name, close to the Santa Lucia church, this welcoming courtyard bar is a classy spot for an evening cocktail, glass of wine, or ice-cold beer.

8 Flamingos, Progreso
MAP C2 ▪ Malecón, corner of Calle 22 ▪ $$

One of Progreso's most enjoyable big terrace bar-restaurants, with tasty ceviches *(see p69)* to go with the beer.

9 Casa Vieja de los Arcos, Campeche
MAP A5 ▪ Calle 10, No. 319, Altos on the plaza ▪ $$

Watch the sun set from the balcony of this Cuban restaurant-bar on Campeche's central square. Enjoy their signature minty Mojitos made with Cuban rum.

10 La Parroquia, Campeche
MAP A5 ▪ Calle 55, No. 8 ▪ $$

Traditional local delicacies are served for breakfast, lunch, and dinner at this popular restaurant with a well-deserved reputation.

Places to Eat

PRICE CATEGORIES

For a three-course meal for one with a beer or soda (or equivalent meal), taxes and extra charges.

$ under $15 $$ $15–$35 $$$ over $35

1 Amaro, Mérida
MAP C2 ▪ Calle 59, No. 507, between Calle 60 and Calle 62 ▪ (999) 928 2451 ▪ $$

One of old Mérida's loveliest patios houses this relaxing restaurant, which has a half-vegetarian menu, including several dishes made with the Yucatecan vegetable *chaya*.

2 El Marlín Azul, Mérida
MAP C2 ▪ Calle 62, No. 488, between Calle 57 and Calle 59 ▪ (999) 928 1606 ▪ $$

Ceviche is the dish to order at this seafood restaurant *(see p70)* but also try the shrimp fajitas. Go for lunch, as it closes at 4pm.

3 El Príncipe Tutul-Xiu, Maní
MAP C4 ▪ Calle 26 No. 208, between Calle 25 and Calle 27 ▪ (999) 929 7721 ▪ $$

Set under a giant *palapa* roof, this restaurant is busiest on Sundays, when families drive from Mérida to eat *poc-chuc*, *panuchos*, and other Yucatecan staples *(see pp68–9)*.

4 La Palapa, Celestún
MAP A3 ▪ Calle 12, by corner of Calle 11 ▪ (988) 916 2063 ▪ $$

Automatic first choice in Celestún, a comfortable beach terrace beneath a *palapa* roof, serving up succulent, coriander-rich platters of octopus, fish, and shrimp.

5 Casa Peón, Celestún
MAP A3 ▪ Calle 12, No. 123 ▪ $

The excellent service at Casa Peón is complemented by the food, which features delectable seafood dishes like crab ceviche. There's also live music, which encourages diners to dance.

6 Hacienda Uxmal, Uxmal
MAP C4 ▪ Antigua Carretera Mérida, Campeche, km 78 ▪ $$$

Located opposite the site of Uxmal, this restaurant has a tropical garden, locally made artworks, and serves fine local and international cuisine.

7 La Chaya Maya, Mérida
MAP C2 ▪ Corner of Calle 62 and Calle 57, between 60 and 62 ▪ $$

An oasis *(see p71)* of high-quality, reasonably priced Yucatecan food, amid its more costly neighbors. Dishes range from *salbutes* to *cochinita pibil (see pp68–9)*.

8 La Pigua, Campeche
MAP A5 ▪ Alemán No. 179A ▪ $$

Taking advantage of Campeche's prime position on the Gulf of Mexico, La Pigua serves fresh fish and seafood in sophisticated surroundings.

Casa de Piedra, Xcanatún

9 Casa de Piedra, Xcanatún
MAP C2 ▪ Xcanatún, 7 miles (12 km) N of Mérida ▪ (999) 941 0213 ▪ $$$

A comfortable hacienda restaurant in a garden, Casa de Piedra *(see p71)* combines local and Caribbean cooking with a few French touches.

10 Hacienda San José Cholul
MAP C2 ▪ Hwy Tixkokob–Tekanto, km 30 ▪ (999) 924 1333 ▪ $$$

Set in a lovely colonial hacienda, the biggest draw is the secluded garden. The service is also excellent.

See map on p108

Streetsmart

Colorful colonial buildings
in Campeche's old walled city

Getting Around	**118**
Practical Information	**120**
Places to Stay	**126**
General Index	**134**
Acknowledgments	**140**
Phrase Book	**142**

Getting Around

Arriving by Air

Frequent direct flights depart on a daily basis from cities across Canada and the US to Cancún and the Yucatán. From the UK or mainland Europe, you generally have to travel via the US or Mexico City, although there are a few scheduled flights, plus several charter services during the high seasons. There are flights between Mexico City and regional airports. Airlines that fly to the area include major carriers such as **Delta Airlines**, **American Airlines**, and **United Airlines**, plus **Aeroméxico**, **Magnicharters**, **Air Europa**, and **Volaris**.

Cancún Airport, 9 miles (15 km) south of the city, near the southernmost point of Cancún Island, is the main international airport in the Yucatán. *Colectivo* minibuses are the easiest means of public transport from the airport to the city. They take an hour, traveling along the Hotel Zone and into Ciudad (Downtown) Cancún, dropping each passenger at their hotel. Airport taxis are another alternative; cab stands can be found just as you exit the airport terminal. If you'd like to reserve transportation in advance, **Happy Shuttle** is one recommended option. When you are departing for the airport, any Cancún city cab can take you there.

There are also public transport services from Cancún airport to various other destinations. The Riviera Maya bus leaves for Puerto Morelos and Playa del Carmen almost hourly between 10:30am and 7pm. There are also hourly *colectivos* from outside the domestic arrivals hall, 6am–6pm. If you're going anywhere else on the coast, take the bus to Playa del Carmen and continue from there.

Both Cozumel and Mérida airports also have international connections. **Cozumel Airport** is just north of San Miguel town; **Mérida Airport** is about 3 miles (4 km) southwest of the city center; taxis and *colectivos* are available from both airports.

Arriving by Road

When driving from the US you will need a Tourist Card to travel beyond the 12-mile (20-km) border zone and stay for more than 72 hours. You should also obtain Mexican insurance and a Temporary Import Permit for your vehicle, which is valid for six months. Allow five days or so to drive from the Texas border to the Yucatán. It's worth noting that most US car-rental companies will not allow their cars to be driven into Mexico. Bear in mind that the US-Mexico border, especially around Ciudad Juárez and Tijuana, is a hotspot in Mexico's drugs war, so it is essential to exercise extra caution. Always refer to government advice *(see p120)* before travelling into the country by car. Indeed, in most instances, it is easier and safer to reach Mexico by plane, unless you're driving from within the country itself.

Buses

Buses are the main form of transport for longer trips in the Yucatán, unless you rent a car or fly. First-class buses are air-conditioned and run between main cities and towns with only a few stops en route. Second-class buses are cheaper, a bit less comfortable, and stop more often. Every city and most towns have a local bus service. Destinations are usually displayed on the windscreen, but **Cancún buses** will show route numbers (routes R-1 and R-2 run up and down the Hotel Zone and to Ciudad Cancún). *Colectivos* (or *combis*) are minibuses that serve the smaller and outlying districts and generally depart when full.

Ferries

Passenger ferries run to Isla Mujeres from Puerto Juárez, which is just north of Cancún, at intervals of every half hour or so daily. Fast boats will get you there in around 20 minutes. There are also several daily car ferries from Punta Sam, north of Puerto Juárez. Shuttle boats run from points along Cancún beach, too.

Passenger ferries operated by **Ultramar** and **Winjet** run roughly every two hours between Playa del Carmen and Cozumel. The journey takes about 45 minutes. A Cozumel shuttle boat runs from

Playa Tortugas or Muelle Fiscal in Cancún.

The car ferry, which runs from Puerto Morelos to Cozumel, is infrequent and expensive.

Taxis

Taxis in Cancún and the Yucatán don't tend to have meters, but instead charge official set rates for each locality. Note that cab drivers in some places, particularly Cancún, Playa del Carmen, and Tulum, have a bad reputation for charging foreigners exaggerated rates.

The complicated official pricing system in Cancún, where there are different prices for the Hotel Zone and Ciudad Cancún, also makes scams easier. In Cancún, the official rates are significantly higher for trips to and from anywhere in the Hotel Zone than in Ciudad Cancún.

Wherever you are going, always agree upon a price before getting into the cab, and firmly refuse any outrageous demands.

Car

A car makes getting to the Mayan sites and more isolated beaches in the region much easier. There are plenty of rental offices along the Riviera Maya, including global agencies **Avis** and **Alamo**, but if you are traveling around the Yucatán, it is best to rent in Mérida, whose smaller agencies tend to charge lower rates. To rent a car you must be over 21 and have your driving license, passport, and a credit card. Jeeps are popular, as some of the more remote roads are unpaved.

Prices are usually higher than in the US but lower than in Europe for both unleaded (*magna* or high-grade premium) and diesel. Occasionally, gas station attendants start the pump with *pesos* already on the gauge. To avoid this, get out of the car and check the pump first. The attendant should then demonstrate that it is set at zero. In rural areas, gas stations are few and far between, so make sure you fill up whenever you can.

There are two fast toll highways in the Yucatán – the 180-Cuota part of the route between Cancún and Mérida, and another stretch from Campeche to Champotón. Tolls are relatively high, so many drivers prefer the parallel old road (180–Libre).

The main peculiarity of driving in Mexico is the *tope*, or speed bump, designed to make the streets safer for pedestrians. Although they are usually signposted, they are very steep and can catch drivers unawares, causing damage to vehicles going at any speed above a crawl.

Night falls very quickly in the tropics, and there is no lighting at all in country areas. *Topes*, potholes, and people on bicycles can rapidly become hazardous.

Walking

Old Yucatán towns like Mérida, Campeche, and Valladolid are fairly compact, and strolling around is the best way to get to know them. Mechanized transport is only really essential in Cancún.

Cycling

Cancún has a dedicated cycle track all along the Hotel Zone, and hotels often have guest bikes. In addition, many of the resorts have golf carts and scooters for hire.

DIRECTORY

ARRIVING BY AIR

Aeroméxico
w aeromexico.com

Air Europa
w aireuropa.com

American Airlines
w aa.com

Cancún Airport
w cancunairport.com

Cozumel Airport
w asur.com.mx/
Contenido/Cozumel

Delta Airlines
w delta.com

Happy Shuttle
w happyshuttle
cancun.com

Magnicharters
w magnicharters.com.mx

Mérida Airport
w asur.com.mx/
Contenido/Merida

United Airlines
w united.com

Volaris
w volaris.com/en

GETTING AROUND BY BUS

Cancún buses
w cancun.travel/en

GETTING AROUND BY FERRY

Ultramar
w ultramarferry.com

Winjet
w winjet.mx

GETTING AROUND BY CAR

Alamo
w alamo.com.mx

Avis
w avis.mx

Practical Information

Passports and Visas

For entry requirements, including visas, consult your nearest Mexican embassy or check the Forma Migratoria Múltiple (**FMM**) website. Citizens of the US, Canada, the UK, Australia, New Zealand, and the Schengen region do not need visas to enter Mexico as tourists for less than 180 days.

All visitors need a valid passport and an FMM (tourist card). It's possible to apply for an FMM for free in advance via the FMM website (remember to print it out and bring it with you). If you haven't organized an FMM card in advance, you'll be handed one onboard your plane. Make sure you keep the card with you, as the law requires that you carry it at all times. It also has to be handed in on leaving the country.

Note that the Instituto Nacional de Migración is in the process of rolling out a digital process that will replace the physical tourist card. Check the FMM website for updates.

Visitors entering by land are also required to pay a *derecho de no inmigrante* (non-immigrant visa) entry fee for stays over seven days.

Government Advice

Now more than ever, it is important to consult governmental advice before travelling. The **UK Foreign, Commonwealth and Development Office**, the **US State Department**, the **Australian Department of Foreign Affairs and Trade** and **Gobierno de Mexico** offer the latest information on security, health, and local regulations.

Customs Information

You can find information on the laws relating to goods and currency taken in or out of Mexico on the **Relaciones Exteriores México** website.

Travel Insurance

We recommend that you take out a comprehensive insurance policy covering theft, loss of belongings, medical care, cancellations, and delays, and read the small print carefully.

If you plan to go scuba diving you may need additional coverage.

Health

Mexico has a good public healthcare system but the best care is in private hospitals in the main cities. You may need to pay for treatment upfront and reclaim the money later from your insurance company. Make sure that you take out comprehensive medical insurance and that you have enough funds to cover the cost of treatment while in Mexico.

The region is home to a number of private clinics, including **Hospital Amerimed** in Cancún and the **Centro Médico de las Américas** in Mérida, both of which employ English-speaking staff. For minor ailments, seek advice from pharmacies *(farmacias)*.

Many are open 24 hours a day in large cities and stock a wide range of medications. In small towns and rural areas, basic public health centers *(centros de salud)* have emergency facilities. It's also a good idea to take a basic first-aid kit with you, including bite cream, antiseptic wipes, and remedies for upset stomachs.

All travelers are advised to seek immunization against typhoid, tetanus, polio, hepatitis A, hepatitis B, diphtheria, and rabies. If you are heading into forest or jungle areas elsewhere in Mexico or Central America, consult your doctor about malaria pills. For information regarding COVID-19 vaccination requirements, check government advice.

The quality of tap water has improved greatly, particularly in Cancún. To be on the safe side, however, it's best to drink only bottled or purified water *(agua purificada)*. To help cut back on single-use plastic, bring a water purifier with you from home.

Mangroves are breeding grounds for mosquitoes, which are most active in the early evening, when they spread into neighboring areas – especially around Sian Ka'an, on Isla Holbox, and around watery areas and cenotes behind the coast near Tankah, Puerto Morelos, and some other points on the Riviera. Although mosquitoes in the Yucatán are not malarial, it is still important to use insect repellent, cover up when outside, and sleep under mosquito nets.

Smoking, Alcohol, and Drugs

You must be 18 to smoke in Mexico. Smoking is prohibited in all public places, whether indoors or outdoors.

You must be 18 to drink or purchase alcohol. It's illegal to walk the streets with an open container of alcohol.

The country has strict drug laws, and being caught in possession of any drug will likely result in serious jail time. Some prescription pharmaceuticals can be regarded as illegal drugs here, so it's important to bring a letter from your doctor or your prescription as proof that these drugs are for prescribed personal use only.

ID

Except for the FMM (see p120), carrying ID is not required by law, but it is advisable to take copies of your passport when traveling between cities by bus, near any Mexican border, or if driving a car since there are frequent police checkpoints.

Personal Security

The Yucatán is generally fairly tranquil, but be wary of pickpocketing and petty crime, especially in Cancún, Mérida, and Playa del Carmen. Use your common sense (such as wearing a money belt) and be alert to your surroundings, and you should enjoy a trouble-free trip. There have been incidences of sexual assault against female travelers in resort areas; avoid walking alone late at night or early in

the morning. In the event of an emergency, dial 911, Mexico's **national emergency number**.

Mexico is a culturally diverse country. As a rule, Mexicans are accepting of all people. Although the conservative influence of the Catholic church remains strong, discrimination on the basis of sexual orientation has been made illegal and the LGBTQ+ community is becoming more prominent. This is especially true in urban areas but there may still be a degree of prejudice in small, rural communities. **Gay Mexico Map** lists LGBTQ+ bars, clubs, and hotels in areas throughout the country, including this region.

In tourist areas there are often kiosks with eager staff buttonholing tourists and asking if they want "information." They are actually selling tours or timeshares, so stick to the official tourist offices (see p123).

Natural Hazards

September to November is when hurricanes are most likely to hit. Mexico has in place extensive anti-hurricane precautions, and many buildings in Cancún and the Riviera have green signs that identify them as an official Refugio Anticiclón, to be used as public hurricane shelter when necessary.

Most waters around the Yucatán are placid, but take special care on the eastern beaches of Isla Mujeres and Cozumel and on the surf beaches of Cancún Island, where the seas are rougher and there can be a fairly

strong undertow. Check the warning flags before swimming (blue is safe; yellow means use caution; red means don't swim).

DIRECTORY

PASSPORTS AND VISAS

FMM
w inm.gob.mx/fmme

GOVERNMENT ADVICE

Australian Department of Foreign Affairs and Trade
w dfat.gov.au/

Gobierno de Mexico
w gob.mx/sre/en

UK Foreign, Commonwealth and Development Office
w gov.uk/foreign-travel-advice

US State Department
w travel.state.gov

CUSTOMS INFORMATION

Relaciones Exteriores México
w consulmex.sre.gob.mx

HEALTH

Hospital Amerimed
Av Plaza las Américas Bonampak, Cancún
((998) 881 3400
w amerimedcancun.com

Centro Médico de las Américas
Calle 54, No. 365, nr Paseo Montejo, Mérida
((999) 926 2111
w merida.cma hospital.mx

PERSONAL SECURITY

National Emergency Number
(911

Gay Mexico Map
w gaymexicomap.com

Travelers with Specific Requirements

Larger hotels and resorts in Cancún and Cozumel often have good wheelchair facilities, but always check before booking. Hotels in older buildings can be difficult to access, but sometimes have suitable first-floor rooms.

Public transportation provision in Mexico for travelers with specific requirements is poor, although there are wheelchair ramps and disabled toilets at Cancún Airport. Buses are rarely wheelchair-accessible, but drivers are usually helpful. Cancún sidewalks have wheelchair ramps at street junctions. Elsewhere you'll find dips in the sidewalk kerb.

Thanks to ramps, the slow ferries to Isla Mujeres are easier to board than the enclosed boats, and the crews are very helpful. For Cozumel, enclosed boats are the only choice from Playa del Carmen, but staff can help.

Of the region's many attractions, eco-parks are generally the easiest to visit. Most Mayan sites have steps and narrow, stony paths, but larger sites, such as Chichén Itzá and Uxmal, have relatively smooth walkways.

In terms of activities, **Yucatek Divers** in Playa del Carmen offers diving courses for travelers with specific requirements, including people who have visual impairments, traumatic brain injuries, or mobility impairments. **Cancún Accesible**, meanwhile, offers tours and transportation.

Other useful resources include the Society for Accessible Travel and Hospitality (**SATH**), **México Accesible**, and **Mobility International USA**.

Time Zone

Quintana Roo state, which includes Cancún and the Riviera, is 5 hours behind GMT year-round. Yucatán and Campeche, which make up the rest of the Yucatán Peninsula, are 5 hours behind GMT in summer and six hours behind GMT in the winter.

Money

Mexico's currency is the peso. The usual symbol for the peso is the same as the dollar sign; prices quoted in US dollars usually have the prefix US$ or suffix USD.

Many businesses on the Riviera also accept USD, and many tourists use only USD during their trip. Note, though, that USD prices usually work out higher than pesos. (The hotel and restaurant listings in this book are given in US dollars.)

Most banks have at least one ATM, although they can be hard to find in rural areas. All tourist areas have numerous small foreign-exchange offices (cambios).

MasterCard and VISA are widely accepted for larger purchases in hotels of mid-range level and above, in stores, and at diving schools; American Express is less popular. Credit cards are essential for car rentals, but some restaurants and most smaller shops don't accept them. Contactless payments are

becoming increasingly common but it is always a good idea to carry small amounts of cash for tips and minor purchases.

A tip of 15–20 per cent is expected in restaurants and bars, and hotel porters and housekeeping will expect a tip of $10–20 per bag or day. At major resort hotels, additional tips are expected: $20–50 per day for housekeeping and $50–100 for the concierge. It is not usual to tip taxi drivers.

Electrical Appliances

Mexico operates on a 110-volt system, as in the US and Canada, and with the same American-type of flatpin plugs. For equipment using 220–240 volts, you will need transformers and plug adaptors.

Mobile Phones and Wi-Fi

To use your cell phone in Mexico, you will need a roaming-enabled quad-band handset – consult your service provider for tariffs. Calls can be expensive so consider purchasing a Mexican SIM card or phone once you've arrived.

High-speed internet is generally widely available throughout Mexico, especially in the cities. Increasingly, cities are providing free Wi-Fi in public spaces, and many cafés, restaurants, and businesses offer free Wi-Fi.

Postal Services

Mexico's postal service is run by **Correos de México**. Main post offices (oficinas de correos) are open from 8am to 8pm on weekdays, and from 8am to 3pm on Saturdays. Smaller ones often have shorter opening hours. **Mexpost** also run a courier service, available at main post offices.

Weather

The Yucatán has tropical weather, with a hot dry season from November to June, and a wet season from June to November. September to November is hurricane season.

Opening Hours

Most shops open around 8:30am and close at 9pm from Monday to Saturday, with the more traditional ones closing for lunch 1–3pm. Markets open very early, before 8am, and close by 2–3pm. Banks are usually open 8:30am–4pm Monday to Friday, and 9am– 1pm on Saturday; some may not exchange money in the afternoons or on Saturdays.

COVID-19 Increased rates of infection may result in temporary opening hours and/or closures. Always check ahead before visiting museums, attractions and hospitality venues.

Visitor Information

There are well-staffed tourist offices in **Cancún**, **Mérida**, **Campeche**, **Playa del Carmen**, **Valladolid**, and **Isla Mujeres**, where you can source information, recommendations, and maps. Useful online resources include **Caribe Mexicano**, **Mexonline. com**, and **Visit Mexico**. Cancún's **Go City** pass offers discounts if you're visiting multiple sights.

Sustainable Travel

When visiting sacred sites always be respectful of local traditions, history,

and culture. Turn off your cell phone and only take photographs (including of people) if permitted.

At the beach, use fully biodegradable and reef-safe sunscreen, to minimize your impact on marine environments.

Another issue affecting the Yucatán Peninsula (and Mexico as a whole) is water scarcity. To help, avoid long showers, and having your room cleaned on a daily basis.

The state of Quintana Roo – which covers much of the east of the Yucatán Peninsula – has introduced a tourist tax, known as the **Visitax**, to help fund infrastructure and tourism-focused projects. The tax is 224 Mexican pesos (roughly $12) per person. It can be paid online before arriving in country, at a resort or in the airport prior to your departure. If paying online, be sure to use the official website listed here.

DIRECTORY

TRAVELERS WITH SPECIFIC REQUIREMENTS

Cancún Accesible
w cancunaccesible.com

México Accesible
w accesiblemexico.com

Mobility International USA
w miusa.org

SATH
w sath.org

Yucatek Divers
w yucatek-divers.com

POSTAL SERVICES

Correos de México
w correosdemexico.com.mx

Mexpost
w gob.mx/correosdemexico

VISITOR INFORMATION

Campeche Tourist Office
Casa Seis, Parque Principal
w campeche.travel

Cancún Tourist Office
Cancún Town Hall, Av Tulum

Caribe Mexicano
w caribemexicano.travel

Go City
w gocity.com

Isla Mujeres Tourist Office
Av Rueda Medina 130

Mérida Tourist Office
Calle 62, Centro Palacio Municipal

Mexonline.com
w mexonline.com

Playa del Carmen Tourist Office
Av Juárez, corner of Av 15

Valladolid Tourist Office
Southeastern corner of town square

Visit Mexico
w visitmexico.com

SUSTAINABLE TRAVEL

Visitax
w visitax.gob.mx/sitiol

Language

Spanish is the official language throughout Mexico, though 68 living Indigenous languages are also spoken in the country. In the Yucatán region, more than half a million residents speak an Indigenous language, with the most common languages being Maya, Ch'ol, Tseltal, and Náhuatl. You are likely to hear one or more of these languages in your travels around the peninsula. English, however, is also spoken widely, particularly in resort areas.

Taxes and Refunds

Prices usually include 16 per cent sales tax, or IVA (Impuesto al Valor Agregado). If a price is given as más IVA (plus sales tax) it means that 16 per cent will be added to the bill. It is possible to claim a refund upon exiting Mexico, so save your receipts if you wish to do this.

Vistors to the state of Quintana Roo are also charged a tourist tax known as the Visitax (see p123).

Trips and Tours

Local travel agencies can be good for unusual tours, diving, forest trips, and so on. Among the best is **Mayan Heritage** in Mérida. Many companies offer guided tours to the main Mayan sites, but few allow more than an hour and a half on-site, and they often arrive all together at the hottest part of the day.

For simple city tours, Mérida's Paseo Turístico bus leaves from Parque Santa Lucía several times daily. In Campeche, the Tranvía de la Ciudad runs bus tours from the Parque Principal, and a trolley, El Guapo, also has trips to the fortress-museums of San José and San Miguel.

Chichén Itzá, Uxmal, and Cobá have official guides, who can show you round for an hourly fee. Able linguists, they are often highly informative, though guides at smaller sites are less likely to be genuinely knowledgeable.

Agencies in the Sian Ka'an Biopshere Reserve (see pp26–7) offer some excellent day tours, and a number of companies, such as **Alltournative**, **Ecoturismo Yucatán**, and **Ecocolors**, specialize in nature and bird-watching trips. Fishers in the Campeche Petenes (see p56) will be able to take you to places you'd never discover without local knowledge, while boaters in both Río Lagartos and Celestún (see p57) run trips to see the flamingos.

Most ecotours are run by small-scale operators, who can be hard to find. Essential resources include the websites of the **Yucatan Wildlife** and **Pronatura** organizations.

Dive shops abound on the Riviera, many of which also offer snorkeling trips, including **Aquatech**, **Phocéa Caribe**, Yucatek Divers (see p122), Aqua World (see p54), and **Squalo Adventures**. Several dive companies, such as the **Cenote Dive Center**, offer cenote tours, with diving or snorkeling, especially around Tulum.

Specialist fishing-trip agencies and fishing lodges get booked up far in advance. For casual fishing, the best places include Isla Mujeres, Cozumel, Isla Holbox, and Puerto Morelos.

Shopping

The Riviera is a great place to find souvenirs. There are malls dedicated to souvenir items in Cancún and Playa del Carmen. Mérida and Campeche, meanwhile, have official handicrafts stores (casas de artesanías), which sell traditional crafts.

Jewelry stores aimed at cruise passengers are a specialty of Cozumel and, to a lesser extent, Isla Mujeres and Cancún. As well as the bling, they sell items made with local jade, amber, and black obsidian. Playa del Carmen and Cancún have a number of stores show-casing quality silver work. Fine embroidery of bright flower patterns on a plain white background is one of the foremost traditional products of the Yucatán, most often seen in the simple huipil blouses of Mayan women but also on items such as hand-kerchiefs and tablecloths. Valladolid and Mérida are the best places to find good embroidery.

Hammocks vary a lot in quality. The toughest ones are 100 per cent cotton. The specialist hammock shops in the market area in Mérida are the best places to look for one.

Panamas make great sunhats, and the best will regain their shape even after being rolled up for packing: head to Mérida market and the small specialist shops nearby.

For tequila, take advantage of the excellent duty-free selection at Cancún Airport. Cheaper and more local Yucatán specialties include fine rums and *xtabentún*, a sweet, herby, traditional Mayan honey drink.

Haggling is accepted in markets, especially for larger items, but it should not be intensive or drawn-out. Many shops offer discounts if you buy more than one of any item.

Dining

As well as *restaurante*, you can eat at a more casual *lonchería* (lunch counter) or *cocina económica* ("budget kitchen"), which offers diners good, simple local cooking.

On most restaurant tables you'll find two little bowls of sauce. The red one is relatively gentle; the green one, made with habanero chilis, blows the head off the uninitiated. Apart from this, Yucatecan dishes are more fragrant than spicy.

Mexicans snack on a frequent basis. Some dishes are small, others big platters of mixed fish, seafood, and salads. They enjoy *comida*, which is traditionally the largest meal of the day and is usually eaten in the afternoon. Vendors in every town and village offer tacos, *tortas* and other *antojitos (see p69)*, ice cream and fruit.

The area has a great range of fresh fruits, such as mangoes, watermelon, and native mamey fruit. Juice shops serve it three ways: as straight juice; a *licuado*, blended with some water or milk; or an *agua*, with water and ice.

Tequila comes from Jalisco, but is found across the Yucatán, and some bars specialize in tastings of their many labels. *Blanco* is the youngest tequila; *reposado* is aged for up to 11 months; darker *añejo* is aged for up to five years. Being largely exported, tequila has become fairly expensive in Mexico itself.

As well as international beer brands, the Yucatán has its own Montejo brewery, with a fine light beer (Montejo Especial) and a great ale, León Negra. Most restaurants have only a small choice of Mexican wines; upscale restaurants usually serve imported US, European, and Chilean wines, at very high prices.

The *cantina* is the most traditional Mexican bar. There used to be laws barring women, but these rules have since been relaxed. You can still find old-style *cantinas* complete with secretive, screened doorways.

Accommodation

The region is home to a wide range of accommodations to suit all budgets, from luxury resorts and hip boutique hotels to family-run guesthouses and economical hostels. **Bookings.com**, **Hotels.com**, and **BestDay.com** are useful for bookings.

Cabañas (cabins), often with kitchens, are a good value, self-catering option for families and groups. *Haciendas* (Spanish-era ranches) are atmospheric, but expensive. Another option is to stay in a private home or villa, booked through sites such as **Homestay.com**, **VRBO**, and **AirBnB**.

Places to Stay

PRICE CATEGORIES

For a standard, double room per night (with breakfast if included), taxes, and extra charges.

$ under $60 $$ $60–$150 $$$ Over $150

Luxury Hotels

Casa de los Sueños, Isla Mujeres

MAP L2 ■ Carretera Garrafón ■ (998) 877 0708 ■ www. hotelcasa suenos.com ■ $$$

This secluded lodge is located toward the southern end of Isla Mujeres. It has ten spacious rooms, a swimming pool, and oceanside terrace, all in contemporary Mexican style. It's stunning and supremely comfortable.

Fiesta Americana Grand Coral Beach, Cancún

MAP L4 ■ Blvd Kukulcán, km 9.5 ■ (998) 881 3200 ■ www.coralbeachcancun resort.com ■ $$$

With cascades of greenery spilling down from its many balconies, the awesomely huge Coral Beach has 602 rooms and a thick catalog of facilities, including tennis courts and its own jogging track, as well as a private beach.

Fiesta Americana, Mérida

MAP C2 ■ Paseo de Montejo 451 ■ (999) 942 1111 ■ www.fiestameri cana.com ■ $$$

Mérida's premier hotel is modern but built in an ornate French-mansion style, with a spectacular stained-glass atrium. Rooms are spacious and well-equipped.

Hacienda Chichén, Chichén Itzá

MAP E3 ■ Carretera Mérida-Puerto Juárez, km 120 ■ (999) 920 8407 ■ www.haciendachichen. com ■ $$$

This place is set in an old colonial hacienda next to the site of Chichén Itzá. Most of the airy rooms are in bungalows used by archaeologists in the 1920s. It's now an award-winning eco-resort and spa, offering organic food and holistic treatments.

Rosas y Xocolate

MAP C2 ■ Paseo de Montejo 480, Zona Paseo Montejo, Centro, Mérida ■ 999 924 2992 ■ www. rosasandxocolate.com ■ $$$

Two restored mansions consist of 17 guest rooms which have pink and chocolate color schemes. All rooms have an outdoor Jacuzzi. There's a restaurant and spa on-site.

Hotel Secreto, Isla Mujeres

MAP L1 ■ Playa Norte ■ (998) 877 1039 ■ www. hotelsecreto.com ■ $$$

Hidden away on the far side of Isla Mujeres, this small hotel is utterly quiet, even though it is located just a few minutes' walk from the center of town. Furnished with four-poster beds, the nine suites overlook the Caribbean. The hotel has a long pool and outdoor "living room" bar.

InterContinental Presidente, Cozumel

MAP R5 ■ Carretera a Chankanaab, km 6.5 ■ (1) 877 660 8550 ■ www.presidente cozumel.com ■ $$$

Big for Cozumel, but smallish by Cancún standards (218 rooms), this is one of the island's longest-established hotels. It enjoys a superb location with its own marina. Diving, snorkeling, and fishing trips can be arranged, but some sections of coral reef are within easy swimming distance of the hotel's long stretch of private, white-sand beachfront.

JW Marriott, Cancún

MAP K5 ■ Blvd Kukulcán, km 14.5 ■ (998) 848 9600 ■ www.marriott.com ■ $$$

This large hotel in Cancún is next door to the same company's slightly older Casa Magna. Expect state-of-the-art facilities, from the lavish health spa to the multitude of electronic accessories in the rooms.

Kempinski Hotel, Cancún

MAP K5 ■ Retorno del Rey 36 ■ (998) 881 0808 ■ www.kempinski.com ■ $$$

Top of the scale for sheer luxury in Cancún, the Ritz Carlton looks like the biggest, grandest Italian Renaissance palace ever built. All 365 rooms have ocean views, balconies, or terraces, and there's a private beach and five restaurants, plus a spa.

Zoëtry Villa Rolandi, Isla Mujeres

MAP L1/2 ■ Fraccion-amiento Laguna Mar ■ (998) 999 2000 ■ www. zoetryresorts.com/ mujeres ■ $$$

A modest-sized hotel, Zoëtry is set on the western side of Isla's Laguna Macax, and has its own beach and boat landing stage, with superb views across to Cancún. No children under 13 are admitted – honeymoons are a specialty. Each balcony has its own Jacuzzi.

Haciendas and Hip Hotels

Hacienda Yaxcopoil, near Mérida

MAP C2 ■ Yaxcopoil village ■ (999) 900 1193 ■ www.yaxcopoil. com ■ $$$

Once one of the region's biggest haciendas, sprawling over some 35 sq miles (90 sq km), Yaxcopoil is an atmospheric place to spend the night. There is a *casa principal* (main house) filled with colonial-era art and furnishings, plus a chapel, a small Mayan museum, along with a delightful guesthouse with en-suite rooms.

Casa Azul, Mérida

MAP C2 ■ Calle 60, No. 343 by 35 and 37 ■ (999) 925 5016 ■ www.casaazulhotel. com ■ $$$

This colonial-era house, named for its rich blue hue, is an exclusive property decorated with period antiques throughout. Guests can experience luxurious amenities and the utmost privacy during their stay. Service is formal but warm.

The Diplomat Boutique Hotel, Mérida

MAP C2 ■ Calle 78, No. 493A by 59 and 59A ■ (999) 117 2972 ■ www.thediplomat merida.com ■ $$$

This colonial-era boutique hotel, run by Canadian expats, has four spacious suites. The original tiles and carefully selected antiques, along with the decor, create an ambience of an earlier era. Knowledgeable and warm service.

Hacienda Puerta Campeche, Campeche

MAP A5 ■ C/59, No. 71 ■ (981) 816 7508 ■ www. puertacampeche.com ■ $$$

A set of 17th-century houses have been transformed into the area's most original hotel. Rooms and suites have satellite TV, and the place also has a restaurant, lounge bar, and pool.

Hacienda San José Cholul, near Mérida

MAP C2 ■ 18 miles (29 km) E of Mérida ■ (999) 924 1333 ■ www.marriott. com ■ $$$

This 17th-century estate is one of several aristocratic haciendas now converted into hotels. Rooms are spacious, with colonial-style furniture. There's an outdoor spa and a swimming pool in the grounds.

Hacienda Santa Rosa, near Mérida

MAP C2 ■ Carretera Mérida Campeche ■ (999) 923 1923 ■ www. marriott.com ■ $$$

Just west of the Mérida to Campeche road, is another hacienda hotel

featuring 11 rooms and suites. The lofty, colonial-style rooms are gorgeous, and some come complete with their own little garden. The gourmet restaurant, bar (located in the estate's old chapel), and pool are in perfect harmony.

Hacienda Temozón, near Uxmal

MAP C4 ■ Carretera Merida-Uxmal ■ (999) 923 8089 ■ www. marriott.com ■ $$$

This hacienda is the most luxurious place to stay near Uxmal, 27 miles (43 km) north of the site. The 17th-century main house, terrace restaurant, and pool are spectacular.

Hacienda Uayamón, Campeche

MAP A5 ■ Carretera Uayamon-China-Edzna ■ (981) 813 0530 ■ www. marriott.com ■ $$$

This is the most isolated of all the Plan haciendas, situated on a former *henequen* (sisal, used for ropemaking) plantation. The conversion has been done with style, and the swimming pool – set in a ruined, roofless building – is astonishing.

Hacienda Xcanatún, near Mérida

MAP C2 ■ Xcanatún, 7 miles (12 km) N of Mérida ■ (999) 930 2140 ■ www. angsana.com ■ $$$

This lovely 18th-century hacienda, five minutes from Mérida, offers 18 suites, each with a terrace and Jacuzzi, in luxuriant gardens. There's a terrace bar, two pools, a spa, and a superb restaurant, the Casa de Piedra, or Stone House *(see p71)*.

Maroma Resort & Spa, Punta Maroma

MAP R4 ▪ Carretera Cancún-Tulum, km 51 ▪ (998) 872 8200 ▪ www. belmond.com ▪ $$$

This retreat is frequented by celebrities attracted to its lush jungle and stretch of private beach. Rooms are vast, and there are three pools plus a choice of restaurants and bars. Beauty-therapy enthusiasts and honeymooners are well catered for.

Resort Hotels

Akumal Bay Beach & Wellness Resort, Akumal

MAP P5 ▪ Carretera Cancun-Chetumal, km 104 ▪ (984) 875 7500 ▪ www.akumalbayresort. com ▪ $$$

This medium-sized resort features a large pool that snakes along beside some of the rooms. It's a short walk from Akumal village along the beach.

Barceló Maya Beach Resort, Puerto Aventuras

MAP Q5 ▪ Carretera Chetumal Puerto Juárez, km 266 ▪ (984) 875 1500 ▪ www.barcelo.com ▪ $$$

This complex is made up of four hotels – the Beach, the Caribe, the Tropical and the Colonial. The idea is that you "stay at one, play at four." Highlights include a nightclub under a giant *palapa* plant and a luxurious beachside buffet.

Club Med Cancún

MAP K6 ▪ Punta Nizuc, Blvd Kukulcán, km 20 ▪ (998) 881 8200 ▪ www. clubmed.com ▪ $$$

This spacious site has the typical Club Med range of

sports facilities – enough even when the 456 rooms fill up – and offers youth-oriented entertainment including a techno disco.

Grand Oasis, Cancún

MAP K5 ▪ Blvd Kukulcán, km 16.5 ▪ (998) 881 7000 ▪ www.grandoasiscancun resort.com ▪ $$$

With 1,320 rooms, this hotel-resort is built on a grand scale. Three giant pyramids make up the main buildings. There are 18 restaurants and bars, and the Up & Down nightclub. The resort's swimming pool is one of Latin America's biggest. Enjoy a vast range of watersports and theme parties.

Iberostar, Cozumel

MAP R6 ▪ San Miguel de Cozumel ▪ (987) 872 9900 ▪ www.iberostar. com ▪ $$$

The 293-room Iberostar faces a fine beach and is well located for diving and snorkeling in the west corner of the island, near Punta Francesa. Like the Tucán *(see p130)*, it offers a wide range of activities.

Hotel Casa Hormiga, Bacalar

Av 3, Calle 32, corner of Mario Villanueva Madrid ▪ (983) 120 5655 ▪ www. casahormiga.com ▪ $$

This environmentally friendly boutique hotel is a magnet for eco-conscious guests. The 18-room property was built with local materials and is surrounded by native flora. Its restaurant, Brote, serves dishes inspired by traditional Mexican and Middle Eastern recipes, all made using locally sourced ingredients, while all

products at its on-site spa are biodegradable and fair-trade.

Moon Palace Golf & Spa Resort, near Cancún

MAP R3 ▪ Carretera Cancún-Chetumal, km 36.5 ▪ (998) 881 6000 ▪ www.moonpalace cancun.com ▪ $$$

The biggest all-inclusive resort of them all, the Moon Palace *(see p82)* has 2,131 luxurious rooms in beach-house style. It offers every possible activity, 14 restaurants, and a 27-hole golf course. It regularly hosts major music and theatrical acts, including Cirque Du Soleil.

Reef Resort, Playacar

MAP Q4 ▪ Av Xaman Ha, Playacar ▪ (984) 873 4120 ▪ www.thereef playacar.com ▪ $$$

A good-value spot when compared to most places, this resort offers an all-meals-included plan. Rooms and food are relatively basic, but it has a great beach location and a fine pool. Its simple style and all inclusive meals have won it many fans.

Royal Hideaway, Playa del Carmen

MAP Q4 ▪ Lote 6, Playacar ▪ (984) 873 4500 ▪ www.barcelo. com ▪ $$$

This all-inclusive, adults-only resort prides itself on its excellent food, with a tempting choice of gourmet Spanish, Asian, and also Italian restaurants. The rooms come with ceiling fans, wicker furniture, and wood porches.

Copal Tulum Hotel
MAP P6 ■ Calle Ixchel, corner of Av Juanek ■ (984) 143 1410 ■ www.copaltulumhotel.com ■ $$$

Covered by tropical foliage, this hotel offers big apartment-like lodgings, with kitchens; some even have their own pools. There's also a spa, a restaurant, and two common pools.

Cabaña Hotels

Sol Caribe, Punta Allen
MAP G5 ■ Via Costera km 35 ■ (984) 876 5896 ■ www.solcaribe-mexico.com ■ $

This clean, simple cabaña has mosquito net-wrapped beds and a restaurant serving Mexican, Italian, and seafood dishes. The staff organize excursions to the nearby Sian Ka'an Biosphere Reserve, as well as fishing, boating, and snorkeling trips.

Coco's Cabañas, Punta Bete
MAP R4 ■ Xcalacoco, Lte 2 ■ (998) 874 7056 ■ www.cocoscabanas.com ■ $

Experience exceptional service at this simple property, with six cozy bungalows. There's a popular on-site restaurant that gets rave reviews.

Cabañas Paamul, Playa del Carmen
MAP Q4 ■ Carretera Federal Cancun-Tulum, km 85 ■ (984) 875 1053 ■ www.paamul.com ■ $$

Spacious beach rooms are set amid a campsite here; some are in a modern building, others in palm-roofed huts. There's a bar-restaurant (see p98), and an uncrowded beach.

Genesis Retreat, Ek-Balam
MAP F2 ■ Off the NE corner of the town plaza ■ (985) 100 4805 ■ www.genesisecooasis.com ■ $$

A beautiful eco-lodge, Genesis is a lush garden set around a bio-filtered pool, with rooms tucked away in the greenery. Bird-watching trips and tours to meet the Mayan neighbors are offered. Food is sourced from a local organic farm.

Xamach Dos, Boca Paila
MAP G4 ■ Beach Road, km 32 ■ (719) 602 9414 ■ www.xamachdos.com ■ $$

This rustic, eco-friendly property features six unique *casitas* (wooden cabins). Its seaside location guarantees amazing views and there is a beautiful open-air restaurant.

Cabañas María del Mar, Isla Mujeres
MAP S1 ■ Av Carlos Lazo 1 ■ (998) 877 0179 ■ www.cabanasmariadelmar.com ■ $$$

A little island of mellow comfort just behind Isla's Playa Norte, with the most popular bar on the beach, Buho's, attached. There's a main building with rooms or cabaña-bungalows; some are on the small side, but they are all attractive. Health treatments and massages are a specialty.

Eco-Paraíso Xixim, near Celestún
MAP A3 ■ Calle 12 Antigua ■ (988) 916 2100, (55) 55 68 8246 ■ www.hotelxixim.com ■ $$$

Standing between coconut groves and a remote beach

north of Celestún, this eco-retreat is best accessed by four-wheel drive. Nature and archaeological guided tours are a specialty, and all cabins have beach terraces.

Mahekal Beach, Playa del Carmen
MAP Q4 ■ C/38 Norte by 5th Av ■ US: (984) 873 0579; Canada: (1) 877 235 4452 ■ www.mahekalbeachresort.com ■ $$$

The ultimate in cabaña luxury, Mahekal has palm-roofed beach lodges with traditional Mexican fittings and five-star comforts. The penthouses in particular are superb.

Papaya Playa, Tulum
MAP G4 ■ Tulum Boca Paila, km 4.5 ■ (1) 984 182 7389 ■ www.papayaplayaproject.com ■ $$$

This long-established cabaña hotel offers everything from a basic sand-floor cabin with a shared bathroom to private villas big enough for a family. Strung out along a wide stretch of uncrowded beach, most of the 80 cabañas have views directly onto the Caribbean Sea.

Rancho Sak Ol, Puerto Morelos
MAP R3 ■ Mz 1 Lt 3, sm 3 ■ (998) 871 0181 ■ www.ranchosakol.com ■ $$$

Equipped with their trademark "hanging beds" – solid beds on ropes that swing – the cabins have a typical beachcomber look. The use of an open kitchen is included, and yoga is offered.

For a key to hotel price categories see p126

Mid-Range Hotels on the Riviera

Amaité Hotel & Spa, Isla Holbox

MAP G1 ■ C/Juárez, on the beach ■ (984) 875 2217 ■ www.amaite hotelholbox.com ■ $$

Just two blocks from the main street, this hotel offers 15 comfortable rooms. The Mexican-style rooms are a real pleasure: the doubles and twins upstairs have balconies; the suites below have kitchenettes and terraces. There's a great restaurant, too.

La Pasión Hotel Boutique, Playa del Carmen

MAP Q4 ■ Calle 10 Norte s/n, Centro ■ (984) 879 3005 ■ $

This charming hotel has an excellent pool, with an abundance of private loungers. Each room has a fridge and mini-bar, and Wi-Fi and parking are free.

Hotel Flamingo, Cozumel

MAP R5 ■ Calle 6 N, No. 81 ■ (987) 872 1264 ■ www.hotelflamingo. com ■ $$

Hotel Flamingo began as a dive hotel and still offers a good range of packages for divers. Even if you're not a scuba nut, it's a comfortable place, with well-cared-for rooms and a bar and rooftop sundeck and lounge.

Ibis Cancún Centro, Cancún

MAP K5 ■ Av Tulum s/n ■ (998) 272 8500 ■ www. ibis.com ■ $$

The Cancún branch of the international chain is a solid, good-value choice amid a sea of overpriced mid-range options. The en-suites are clean and comfortable, the staff are efficient, and the hotel's downtown location is convenient for transport connections (including the airport). There is a mini-supermarket next to the hotel entrance.

Mom's Hotel, Playa del Carmen

MAP Q4 ■ Av 30, by C/4 ■ (984) 873 0315 ■ $$

Texan Ricco Merkle's long-running hotel is, as its name suggests, a welcoming home-from-home. The rooms have been going a few years but are comfortable and pretty, and there's a tiny pool in the courtyard, plus a rooftop bar that's a great place for meeting up with people.

Plaza Caribe, Cancún

MAP J3 ■ Av Tulum 19, corner of Av Uxmal ■ (998) 884 1377 ■ www. hotelplazacaribe.com ■ $$

This large hotel's main selling point is that it is right opposite the bus station in Ciudad Cancún, and so is always popular. Despite being in such a traffic-heavy area, it's surprisingly peaceful inside, with attractive and comfortable rooms, pretty gardens, a pleasant pool, a gym, and dining on-site.

Villa Kiin, Isla Mujeres

MAP L1 ■ C/Zazil-Ha, No. 129, Playa Norte ■ (998) 877 1024 ■ www. villakiin.com ■ $$

This villa has a variety of rooms, some of which are like separate little beach houses. All rooms are comfortable and furnished with Mexican textiles. Villa Kiin is in a delightful location, facing the placid Playa Secreto lagoon; snorkel gear is available for guests' use.

Piedra Escondida, Tulum

MAP P6 ■ Tulum Ruinas, Boca Paila Rd, km 3.5 ■ (984) 100 1443 ■ www. piedraescondida.com ■ $$$

Nine rooms, in two-story cabaña-style beach huts, all with decent showers and entrancing views. The restaurant serves a range of Italian and Mexican food.

Villas de Rosa Beach Resort, Akumal

MAP P5 ■ Carrt. Puerto Aventuras–Akuma, km 115 ■ (984) 875 9020 ■ www.cenotes.com ■ $$$

Owners Nancy and Tony de Rosa are the foremost cave-diving specialists on the Riviera, and many of their guests come here to dive. The hotel is also well equipped for families.

Mid-Range Hotels Elsewhere

Casa Hamaca, Valladolid

MAP E3 ■ Parque San Juan, C/49, No. 202A at C/40 ■ (985) 100 4272 ■ www.casahamaca.com ■ $$

This large guesthouse, with its tree-shaded garden, has a countryside feel. It offers not just comfortable beds, but also full spa services and healthy breakfasts.

Eclipse, Mérida
MAP C2 ■ Calle 57, No.
491 ■ (999) 923 1600
■ www.hoteleclipse
merida.com.mx ■ $$
Unlike most hotels in
the city, the Eclipse is
strikingly modern.
Rooms are bright and
breezy, and each one
has a themed mural
(Andy Warhol, Las Vegas,
Zen, and Cinema are
some styles). There's a
small swimming pool,
and the location is con-
venient for the city's
main attractions.

Ecotel Quinta Regia, Valladolid
MAP E3 ■ C/40,
No. 160A, between
C/27 and C/29 ■ (985)
856 3476 ■ www.ecotel
quintaregia.com.mx
■ $$
Neo-colonial in style,
this hotel combines a
colorful Mexican look
with modern facilities.
Lush gardens are over-
looked by the best rooms.
There is a secluded pool,
and the restaurant
makes use of seasonal
garden produce.

Hacienda Uxmal, Uxmal
MAP C4 ■ Highway
Merida Cancun, km
120 ■ (997) 976 2040
■ www.mayaland.com
■ $$
This hacienda is
part of a small chain
of hotels located at
some of the ancient
Mayan sites. All are
built in old-Mexican,
hacienda style, com-
plete with charming
rooms and lush and
well-tended gardens.
The Uxmal branch
offers exceptional
value for money.

Hotel Baluartes, Campeche
MAP A5 ■ Av 16 de
Septiembre 128 ■ (981)
816 3911 ■ www.
baluartes.com.mx ■ $$
Campeche has only a
limited selection of hotels.
This lofty 1970s building
on the seafront is more
comfortable than most.
Be sure to ask for a room
with a sea view to catch
the magnificent sunsets
over the Gulf of Mexico.

Doralba Inn, Chichén Itzá
MAP E3 ■ Hwy 180,
2 miles (3 km) E of
Chichén Itzá ■ (985)
858 1555 ■ www.dolo
resalba.com ■ $$
The best-value place to
stay near Chichén, this
roadside hotel has 40
bright and comfortable
bungalow rooms, a res-
taurant, and two pools.
Mérida has a sister hotel
of the same name – don't
confuse the two when
booking your stay.

Hotel El Mesón Marqués, Valladolid
MAP E3 ■ C/39, No. 203,
Parque Principal ■ (985)
856 2073 ■ www.meson
delmarques.com ■ $$
Valladolid's classic hotel is
in one of its finest old colonial houses, with rooms
set around elegant patios.
There's a great restaurant
(see p107) and a pool.

Hotel Marionetas, Mérida
MAP C2 ■ C/49, No. 516,
between C/62 & C/64
■ (999) 928 3377 ■ www.
hotelmarionetas.com
■ $$
Once a puppet theater, the
beautiful colonial building
that forms the core of this
hotel has rooms painted in
pastel shades with rustic
ceramics. The hotel has a
large pool, and staff serve
a delicious breakfast.

Hotel San Felipe, San Felipe
MAP E1 ■ C/9, between
C/14 and C/16 ■ (986)
862 2027 ■ $$
Staying near Río Lagartos
used to be a problem, so
this hotel is a welcome
arrival. The waterside restaurant serves the catch of
the day, and all the rooms
have sitting areas. Ask for
a lagoon-view balcony.

La Misión de Fray Diego, Mérida
MAP C2 ■ C/61, No. 524,
between C/64 and C/66
■ (999) 924 1111 ■ www.
lamisiondefraydiego.com
■ $$
This grand 17th-century
former monastery has
been converted with a mix
of antiques and modern
bathrooms, a pool, and
other services. Some
rooms have a Spanish-
mansion air; others are
a little less exciting, and
prices vary accordingly.

Guesthouses and B&Bs

Amar Inn, Puerto Morelos
MAP R3 ■ Av Rojo Gómez
■ (998) 871 0026 ■ www.
amarinn.mx ■ $$
This seafront B&B has
lovely views and offers its
guests a delightfully rustic
atmosphere. The decor is
very traditional and each
room has been painted
a different color. The inn
can arrange tours to
nearby tourist spots. This
is just the right place for
travelers looking for a
welcoming and homey
spot typical of the region.

For a key to hotel price categories see p126

Amigo's Hostel, Cozumel

MAP R5 ▪ Calle 7 Sur, No. 571, between Av 30 and 25, Centro, Cozumel ▪ (987) 872 3868 ▪ www. cozumelhostel.com ▪ $$

This hostel offers two large mixed dormitories and one private room with a kitchenette and private terrace, all set around a pool and lovely garden. The place is especially suited to family groups: breakfasts are included and are served in a garden *palapa* or in a palm-roofed gazebo.

Casa del Maya B&B, Mérida

MAP C2 ▪ C/66, No. 410A, between C/45 and C/47 Centro ▪ (1) 999 181 1880 ▪ www. casadelmaya.com ▪ $$

Once the home of an old Mérida family, this 19th-century house has been delightfully restored with six charming, lofty-ceilinged rooms and a *casita* (little house). There's also a lovely garden and pool on the premises. Breakfast on the terrace includes home-baked cinnamon rolls.

Casa Mexilio, Mérida

MAP C2 ▪ C/68, No. 495, between C/59 and C/57 ▪ (999) 928 2505 ▪ www. casamexilio.com ▪ $$

Set in a fine old building, the Casa Mexilio is a special guesthouse. The hallways and seven rooms have traditional furniture and antiques, including some four-poster beds, and the owners, who are Mexican-American, have added many original touches, including a magical, fern-bedecked swimming pool.

La Casa del Mago, Uxmal

MAP C4 ▪ Antigua Carretera Mérida-Campeche km. 78 ▪ (997) 976 2032 ▪ $

Uxmal archaeological site is just a one-minute walk from this property. The pool, bicycles, parking, and Wi-Fi are all included in the room rate. Staff can arrange birdwatching and horseback day trips.

Julamis, Mérida

MAP C2 ▪ Calle 53, No. 475B ▪ (999) 924 1818 ▪ www.hoteljulamis.com ▪ $$

This is an award-winning, adults-only guesthouse. Each of the nine immaculate rooms has been decorated in a different style, but all are elegant and comfortable. Mini-fridges stocked with free beer, water, and soft drinks are a nice touch.

Luz en Yucatán, Mérida

MAP C2 ▪ C/55, No. 499, between C/58 and C/60 ▪ (999) 924 0035 ▪ www. luzenyucatan.com ▪ $$

Once part of a convent, this house is now a quirky and charming urban retreat featuring a lovely pool and modern apartments at bargain prices.

Macan ché, Izamal

MAP D2 ▪ C/22, No. 305, between C/33 and C/35 ▪ (988) 954 0287 ▪ www. macanche.com ▪ $$

Izamal is a tranquil town in any case, but the pretty walled garden, within which hides this B&B, is especially soothing. The little bungalows are dotted about the garden, each imaginatively decorated; one has a kitchen.

Posada Sirena, Punta Allen

MAP G5 ▪ Fax (984) 139 1241 ▪ www.casasirena. com ▪ $$

Punta Allen is about the most beachcomberish destination imaginable, and this guesthouse hits the appropriate note, with a stay-as-long-as-you-want feel from owner Serena, a real character. The four cabins each have their own kitchen and the obligatory hammocks. She can also arrange fishing and diving trips.

Tamarindo, Cozumel

MAP R5 ▪ Calle 4 Norte, No. 421, between 20 and 25 ▪ (987) 872 3614 ▪ www.tamarindobedand breakfast.com ▪ $$

A stylish property, with a sheltered garden, run by Mexican-French owners. Each of the five pretty rooms has its own character, there's an open kitchen and ample breakfasts, and they have many happy clients. They also run Palapas Amaranto nearby, which offers self-contained suites ideal for families or friends.

Budget Accommodations

Hotel La Candelaria, Valladolid

MAP E3 ▪ C/35, No. 201F, between C/42 and C/44 ▪ (985) 856 2267 ▪ www. hostelvalladolidyucatan. com ▪ $

Set in a pretty, old house, this hostel offers excellent, bright dormitory rooms, shared bathrooms, and a generous breakfast. There's also a lounge and a hammock-strung garden for the use of guests.

El Jardin de Frida, Tulum

MAP G4 ▪ Av Tulum s/n Manzana ▪ (984) 871 2816 ▪ www.fridas tulum.com ▪ $

Frida Kahlo lives on at this colorful, budget-friendly hostel, where private rooms, suites, and dorm options are all available. Eat at the on-site restaurant or cook your own meals in the common kitchen. Free Wi-Fi, a garden, and a library are part of the offerings.

Hostel Quetzal, Cancún

MAP J3 ▪ Orquideas 10, Mz 14 ▪ (998) 883 9821 ▪ www.hostelquetzal. com ▪ $

Centrally located, this popular hostel offers both private and dormitory-style rooms with air-conditioning, and with en-suite bathrooms. Breakfast and dinner are included in the cost and there are nightly cocktail parties.

Hotel Carmelina, Isla Mujeres

MAP L1 ▪ Isla Town, between Av Abasolo and Av Guerrero ▪ (998) 877 0006 ▪ $

This place welcomes budget travelers. Set around a big patio, its rooms are simple and cheerful. All have showers, air-conditioning, ceiling fans, and mini-fridges.

Hotel Pepita, Cozumel

MAP R5 ▪ Av 15A Sur, No. 120 ▪ (987) 872 0098 ▪ www.hotelpepita cozumel.com ▪ $

Friendly, helpful owners make the difference in this big, popular hotel. Rooms are well cared for and have air-conditioning and small fridges. Complimentary coffee is provided.

Nómadas Hostel, Mérida

MAP C2 ▪ C/62, No. 433, by C/51 ▪ (999) 924 5223 ▪ www.nomadastravel. com ▪ $

Challenging the cheap hotels of Mérida for value, this hostel has bright, airy dorm rooms as well as 20 private doubles. There's also an open kitchen, a lounge space, and cheap Internet access.

Tribu Hostel, Isla Holbox

MAP G1 ▪ Av Pedro Joaquin Coldwell s/n ▪ (984) 875 2507 ▪ www. tribuhostel.com ▪ $

One of the best hostels in the region, Tribu has well-maintained dorms and private rooms, as well as a hammock-strewn garden, roof terrace, lively bar, and kitchen for guests to use. Movie nights, barbecues, salsa dances, Spanish classes, yoga, and kite-surfing are among the many activities on offer.

Hotel Casa del Balam, Mérida

MAP C2 ▪ Calle 60, No. 468 ▪ (999) 924 8844 ▪ www.casadelbalam. com ▪ $$

One of the oldest hotels in Mérida, Casa del Balam retains its erstwhile charm, thanks in part to its tranquil courtyard. Rooms are spacious with air-conditioning and bright decor. There's a good on-site restaurant, and the hotel is also located near some of the major sights of Centro. Guests can enjoy a homely ambience and attentive service.

Hotel Rinconada del Convento, Izamal

MAP D2 ▪ Calle 33, No. 294 ▪ (988) 954 0151 ▪ www.hotel izamal.com ▪ $$

Centrally located, this hotel is within walking distance of major attractions and restaurants. Rooms have minimal decor and are furnished with basic necessities, making this a good base for those who wish to go out and explore. Some rooms offer views. Guests can relax in the garden or enjoy themselves at the pool.

Popol Vuh, Playa del Carmen

MAP Q4 ▪ C/2, between Av 5 and the beach ▪ No air-conditioning in some rooms; no en-suite ▪ (984) 803 2149 ▪ www.popol-vuh.hotelsplayadel carmen.net/en ▪ $$

A survivor from Playa's hippy days, clinging on to its great beach location in the face of glossier developments. Set inside two garden enclosures are simple cabañas (with or without showers), a private room, and a shared dormitory.

Rancho Sak-Ol, Puerto Morelos

MAP R3 ▪ Mz 1 Lt 3 SM 3 ▪ (998) 169 4834 ▪ www. ranchosakol.com ▪ $

This beachfront budget accommodation offers 13 rooms and a junior suite, each with a terrace, hammock, and private bath. Use of the on-site communal kitchen is also included, as are five-gallon bottles of water (refilled daily), a continental breakfast, use of bikes, and snorkeling equipment.

For a key to hotel price categories see p126

General Index

Page numbers in **bold** refer to main entries.

A

Acamaya 82
Acanceh 49, 112
Accommodations 125–33
  budget accommodations 132–3
  cabaña hotels 129
  guesthouses and B&Bs 131–2
  haciendas and hip hotels 127–8
  luxury hotels 126–7
  mid-range hotels 130–131
  resort hotels 128–9
Admission charges 73
Air tours 61
Air travel 118, 119
Aké 45, 101
Aktun-Chen Cave 94
Aktun-Ha Cenote (Tulum) 22, 94
Akumal 50–51, 52, 63, 92, 95
  accommodations 128, 130–131
  places to eat 99
All Saints' Day 75
Altar of the Red Jaguar (Chichén Itzá) 30
Angelfish 53
Aqua World (Cancún) 56
Arch (Uxmal) 34
Arch of Labná (Labná) 37, 108, 109
Arroz con pulpo 69
Ascension Bay Bonefishing Flats (Sian Ka'an) 27
ATMs 122
Avenida Tulum (Cancún) 12
Aviary (Xcaret) 18

B

B&Bs 132
Balankanché Caves 58, 100
Ball courts 31
  Great Ball Court (Chichén Itzá) 28, 30, 31
  Uxmal 35
  Xcaret 19
Ball game 31
Baluarte de Santiago (Campeche) 39

Banking 122
Barracudas 53
Bars
  discounts 73
  see also Drinking and entertainment spots; Nightlife
Batey (Tulum) 66, 97
Beaches 50–51
  Cancún and the North 83
  Cozumel and the South 95
  safety 121
Ben-Ha Cenote (Sian Ka'an) 27
Bird-watching 56–7
Birds Quadrangle (Uxmal) 36
Blue Lagoon (Xcaret) 18
Boca Paila (Sian Ka'an) 26, 61, 94
  accommodations 129
Bocas de Dzilam 57, 104
Budget accommodations 133
Budget tips 73
Bus travel 73, 118, 119
Butterfly Garden (Xcaret) 18

C

Cabañas (cabins) 125, 129
Cafés *see* Drinking and entertainment spots
Calakmul 31, 38, 109
Calcehtok Caves 59
Calotmul 104
Camarón al mojo de ajo 69
Campeche 11, **38–9**, 49, 109, 116–17
  accommodations 127, 131
  churches 47
  itineraries 7
  places to eat 7, 71, 114, 115
  shopping 113
Cancún 10, **12–13**, 79
  accommodations 13, 126, 128, 130, 133
  beaches 12, 50, 79, 83
  drinking and entertainment 86
  festivals 74
  fishing 61
  itineraries 6–7, 81
  nightlife 13, 66–7, 85
  places to eat 70, 87
  reefs 53
  shopping 12
Cancún Jazz Festival 74

Cancún and the North 78–87
  beaches 83
  Cancún to Tulum tour 81
  drinking and entertainment 86
  map 78
  nightlife 85
  places to eat 87
  shopping 84
  sights 79–82
Canibal Royal (Playa del Carmen) 16
Cantón, General Francisco 33
Car rental 73, 119
Car travel 119
Carlos'n Charlie's (Cozumel) 66, 97
Carnival 73, 74
Casa Colorada (Chichén Itzá) 30
Casa de Piedra (Xcanatún) 71, 115
Casa Seis (Campeche) 38
Caste War 43, 104
Castillo de Kukulcán (Chichén Itzá) 7, 8–9, 28–9, 30
Cathedrals
  Campeche 38, 47
  Mérida 32, 47, 73
  Valladolid 48
Catherwood, Frederick 110
Caves 58–9
  Aktun-Chen Cave 94
  Balankanché Caves 58, 100
  Calcehtok Caves 59
  Loltún Caves 59, 111
  Sleeping Sharks Cave (Isla Mujeres) 20
  see also Cenotes; Diving and snorkeling
Celestún 51, 57, 63, 109
  accommodations 129
  places to eat 115
Cenotes 23, **58–9**, 112
  Aktun-Ha Cenote (Tulum) 22, 94
  Ben-Ha Cenote (Sian Ka'an) 27
  Cenote Xlacah (Dzibilchaltún) 59, 110
  Cenote Yokdzonot 104
  Chichén Itzá 29
  Dos Ojos Cenote (Tulum) 23, 54, 58, 94
  Dzitnup Cenote 59, 101

Cenotes (cont.)
Gran Cenote (Tulum)
23, 59, 94
Ik Kil Cenote 104
Kantun-Chi 58, 82
Sacred Cenote (Chichén
Itzá) 29, 58
Samula Cenote 58, 101
Sian Ka'an 27
Tulum 22, 23
Central Heartland, The
100–107
drinking and
entertainment 106
map 100–101
places to eat 107
shops, markets, and
tours 105
sights 100–104
Two-Day Tour 103
Ceramics 75
shopping 96, 113
Ceviche 69
Chac (god of rain) 43,
110
Chac-Masks of Las Monjas
(Chichén Itzá) 30
Chac Mool (Chichén Itzá)
30
Chakah bushes 27
Chak, Lord 35, 36
Chechen trees 27
Chelem 112
Chen Rio (Cozumel) 14,
93, 95, 99
Chichén Itzá 8–9, 11,
28–31, 102
accommodations 103,
126, 131
carvings 24–5, **30**
handicrafts market 105
itineraries 6, 7, 103
places to eat 106
salt 103
Chicle 80
Children's attractions
64–5
Chunzubul Beach (Playa del
Carmen) 16, 53, 83
Churches 46–7
Guadalupe Chapel 21
Iglesia de Jesús (Mérida)
33, 47
La Mejorada (Mérida) 46
Las Monjas (Mérida) 47
San Antonio de Padua
(Izamal) 46
San Bernardino Sisal
(Valladolid) 46, 72, 103
San Roque (Campeche)
47
Tekax 47
see also Cathedrals;
Monasteries and convents

Climate 122–3
Clinics 120
Cobá 45, 92, 93
Cochinita pibil 68
Coco Bongo (Cancún) 67,
85
Cócteles 69
Codz Poop (Palace of Masks)
(Kabah) 37, 44, 110
Conoco 95
Conquistadores 42
Coralina Daylight Club
17, 85
Coral reefs 52–3
Cozumel 14, 15, 52,
53, 92–3
Isla Mujeres 21, 52
Xel-Ha (Tulum) 23
Xpu-Ha 53, 93, 95
see also Diving and
snorkeling
Cortés, Hernán 91
Cosmic Turtle 43
Court of the Thousand
Columns (Chichén
Itzá) 29
Cousteau, Jacques 14
COVID-19 120, 123
Cozumel 10, **14–15**, 91
accommodations 14, 128,
130, 132, 133
beaches 14, 15, 50, 95
drinking and
entertainment 98
festivals 74
fishing 61
itineraries 7, 93
nightlife 66, 97
places to eat 99
reefs 14, 15, 52, 53, 92–3
shopping 96
Cozumel and the South
90–99
beaches 95
Cozumel in a Day tour 93
drinking and
entertainment 98
map 90–91
nightlife 97
places to eat 99
shopping 96
sights 91–4
Crafts
beadwork 20
Izamal 72
shopping for 84, 96,
105, 113
traditional crafts and
products 75
Crepas de chaya 69
Cristo de las Ampollas
(Mérida) 75
Crococún Crocodile
Park 64, 82

Currency 122
Customs regulations 120
Cycling 61

D
Dady'O (Cancún) 67
Day of the Dead 75
Diablito Cha Cha Cha (Playa
del Carmen) 7, 67, 86
Dinner cruises (Cancún) 66
Discount coupons 73
Discover Mexico Park 55
Diving and snorkeling
52–3, 60
Akumal 51, 52, 92
Cancún 53
cave-diving 52, 58, 59, 94
Cozumel 14, 52, 53, 92–3
discounts 73
Isla Mujeres 21
Playa del Carmen and
Chunzubel 53
Puerto Morelos 50, 52,
56
safety 121
Tankah 52
Tulum 23, 52
Underground Snorkeling
River (Xcaret) 19
Xcaret 18, 19
Xel-Ha 55, 65, 92
Xpu-Ha 53, 93
Dos Ojos Cenote (Tulum)
23, 54, 58, 94
Drinking and entertainment
spots
Cancún and the North
86
Central Heartland 106
Cozumel and the South
98
West, The 114
Dwarf (Uxmal) 35
Dzibilchaltún 44, 59, 110
Dzitnup Cenote 59, 101

E
Earth Lord 43
Eco-parks and theme
parks 54–5
Aktun-Chen 55
Aqua World (Cancún)
54
Discover Mexico Park
55
Dos Ojos Cenote (Tulum)
23, 54, 58
Kantun-Chi 58
Laguna Chankanaab
(Cozumel) 14, 54, 65
Parque Garrafón (Isla
Mujeres) 21, 54
Punta Sur Eco Beach Park
(Cozumel) 15, 57, 93

Eco-parks and theme parks (cont.)
Ventura Park (Cancún) 13, 54, 64, 82
Xcaret 17, **18–19**, 55, 64, 81
Xel-Ha (Tulum) 23, 45, 55, 65
Xplor 54–5, 80–81
Edzná 39, 45, 112
Ek-Balam 44, 102, 103
accommodations 129
places to eat 107
El Bajo 104
El Castillo (Tulum) 23, 76–7
El Cuyo 61, 63, 104
places to eat 106
Electrical appliances 123
El Garrafón (Isla Mujeres) 21, 54
El Marlín Azul (Mérida) 6, 70, 115
Embroidery 75, 84, 105, 113
Emergency services 121
Enchiladas 69
Entertainment *see* Drinking and entertainment spots
Equinoxes 74
Equinox "Descent" (Chichén Itzá) 29

F
Fajitas 69
Fan corals 53
Feast of the Three Kings (Tizimín) 74
Ferries 118–19
Festivals 74–5
Fish 53
Fishing 60, 61
Flamingos 57, 103, 105, 109
Food and drink
dishes of the Yucatán 68–9
menu decoder 144
snacks and street foods 69
where to eat 124–5
see also Drinking and entertainment spots; Restaurants
Forest Trail (Xcaret) 19
Franciscans 46, 47
Free attractions 72–3
Fuerte San José (Campeche) 39
Fuerte San Miguel (Campeche) 38

G
Gift shops 84, 105
Gods and spirits, Mayan 43
Golf 60
Governor's Palace (Uxmal) 35, 36
Gran Cenote (Tulum) 23, 59, 94
Gran Museum del Mundo Maya (Mérida) 32
Great Pyramid (Uxmal) 34
Guayaberas 75
Guesthouses 125, 132
Guides 124

H
Hacienda Chichén (Chichén Itzá) 103, 106, 126
Hacienda Henequenera 18
Hacienda hotels 63, 125, 127–8
Hammocks 75
Hartwood (Tulum) 70, 81, 99
Health 120, 121
Henequén Boom 43
Hernández de Córdoba, Francisco 42
Hero Twins 43
High Priest's Grave (Chichén Itzá) 28
Hip hotels 127–8
History 42–3
Hostels 125
Hotels 125, 126–31
cabaña 129
haciendas and hip 127–8
luxury 126–7
mid-range 130–31
resort 128–9
House of the Old Woman (Uxmal) 35
House of the Pigeons (Uxmal) 34
House of the Turtles (Uxmal) 35
Hurricanes 121, 123

I
Ik Kil Cenote 104
Independence 43
Inoculations 120
Insurance 120
Internet access 122
Isla Contoy 21, 56, 80, 103
Isla Holbox 51, 61, 63, 79, 83
accommodations 130
places to eat 87
Isla Mujeres 7, 10, **20–21**, 80
accommodations 126, 127, 129, 130, 133
beaches 20, 50, 83

Isla Mujeres (cont.)
drinking and entertainment 86
fishing 61
places to eat 87
shopping 84
Isla Town (Isla Mujeres) 20
Itineraries
A Day in the Puuc Hills 111
Cancún to Tulum 81
Central Heartland Two-Day Tour 103
Cozumel in a Day 93
Four Days in Cancún and the Yucatán 6–7
Two Days in Cancún and the Yucatán 6
Itzamná 43
Ixchel 43
Izamal 7, 46, 48, 88–9, 103
accommodations 132, 133
bars 106
crafts workshops 72
market 105
places to eat 70, 107

J
Jewelry 75
shops 84, 96, 105
Jicaras (gourds) 75
Jungle tours 61

K
Kabah 37, 44, 110
Kantun-Chi 58, 82
Kayaking 60
Kinich (Izamal) 70, 107
Kukulcán 30, 43
Ku'uk (Mérida) 71

L
Labná 37, 44, 109, 111
La Caleta Cove (Xcaret) 18
La Candelaria 74
La Chaya Maya (Mérida) 7, 71, 115
Lafitte, Jean and Pierre 21
Laguna Chankanaab (Cozumel) 14, 54, 65, 93
Laguna Nichupté (Cancún) 13
Laguna Yal-Ku (Akumal) 65, 92
La Habichuela (Cancún) 6, 70, 87
Lake Chunyaxché (Sian Ka'an) 26
Lake Islands (Sian Ka'an) 26
Language 142–4
La Parrilla (Cancún) 70, 87
La Picota (Uxmal) 36

La Pigua (Campeche) 7, 71, 115
Las Palmeras (Cozumel) 93, 98
Loltún Caves 59, 111
Los Pelícanos (Puerto Morelos) 70, 81, 87
Luxury hotels 126–7

M
MACAY (Museo de Arte Contemporáneo de Yucatán) (Mérida) 72
Maize God 43
Malaria 120
Malecón, The (Campeche) 38
Malls 84, 96
Mamita's Beach Club (Playa del Carmen) 6, 16, 86
Manchones Reef (Isla Mujeres) 21, 52
Mandala, Playa del Carmen 66, 85
Mangroves 27, 56, 112
Maní 46, 49
  places to eat 115
Markets
  Cancún 81, 84, 87
  Central Heartland 105
  food stalls 73, 87
  Handicrafts Market (Chichén Itzá) 105
  Izamal 105
  Mérida 33, 113
  Oxkutzcab 73
  Tizimín 105
  Valladolid Crafts Market and Bazaar 105
  West,The 113
Mayan civilization 42, 44–5
  Acanceh 49, 112
  Aké 45, 101
  Calakmul 31, 38, 109
  Chichén Itzá 8–9, 11, **28–31**, 44, 102
  Cobá 45, 92, 93
  Dzibilchaltún 44, 110
  Edzná 39, 45, 112
  Ek-Balam 44, 102, 103
  El Meco Site (Cancún) 13, 45, 82
  El Rey Site (Cancún) 13, 45, 81, 82
  gods and spirits 43
  Gran Museo del Mundo Maya (Mérida) 6, 7, 12, 32
  Kabah 37, 44, 110
  Labná 37, 44, 109, 111
  Lake Islands (Sian Ka'an) 26
  Mayan Village and Ball Court (Xcaret) 19

Mayan civilization (cont.)
  Mayapán 45, 112
  Muyil Site (Sian Ka'an) 26, 45, 94
  Oxkintok 45, 112
  Puuc cities **37**
  San Gervasio (Cozumel) 15, 45, 91, 93
  Sayil 37, 44, 110, 111
  Tulum 6–7, 10, 22–3, 45, 91
  Uxmal 11, **34–7**, 45, 64, 109
  Xaman-Ha Mayan Site (Playa del Carmen) 17
  Xcambó 45, 104
  Xel-Ha Site 94
  Xlapak 37, 45, 73, 111, 112
Mayapán 45, 112
Media Luna Bay (Akumal) 65, 90, 92, 95
Medical care 120, 121
Menu decoder 144
Mérida 11, **32–3**, 49, 110–111
  accommodations 126, 127, 131, 132, 133
  churches 46–7
  drinking and entertainment 114
  festivals 40–41, 75
  itineraries 6, 7, 111
  nightlife 67, 72
  places to eat 6, 70, 71, 115
  shopping 113
Mérida en Domingo 40–41, 75
Mestizos 43
Mexican Revolution 43
Monasteries and convents
  Maní Monastery 46
  San Antonio (Izamal) 88–9, 103
Money 73, 122
Monstermouth temples 36, 43, 44
Montejo, Francisco 33
Moon Palace Golf & Spa Resort 82, 128
Morgan, Henry 39
Mosquitoes 120
Museums and galleries
  Fuerte San José Museum (Campeche) 39
  Fuerte San Miguel Museum (Campeche) 38
  Gran Museo del Mundo Maya (Mérida) 6, 7, 12, 32, 81
  MACAY (Museo de Arte Contemporáneo de Yucatán) (Mérida) 72

Museums and galleries (cont.)
  Museo de Antropología (Mérida) 33
  Museo Casa Montejo (Mérida) 32
  Museo de Cozumel (San Miguel) 14
  Museo Subacuático de Arte (Cancún) 6, 7, 12
  Palacio Centro Cultural (Campeche) 38, 72

N
Newspapers 122, 123
Nightlife 66–7
  Cancún 13, 66–7, 85
  Cancún and the North 85
  Cozumel and the South 97
  Mérida 67, 72
  Playa del Carmen 17, 66–7, 85
  Xcaret 19
North Beach (Tulum) 95
Nunnery (Chichén Itzá) 28
Nunnery Quadrangle (Uxmal) 35, 36, 109

O
Observatory (Chichén Itzá) 28
Off the beaten path 62–3
Old Chichén (Chichén Itzá) 29
Olmecs 42
Opening hours 122–3
Orchid Greenhouse (Xcaret) 19
Oxkutzcab 49
  market 73
Oxkintok 45, 112

P
Paamul 94, 95, 98
Pacheco, Fernando Castro 32
Painted birds/ornaments 75
Palacio Centro Cultural (Campeche) 38, 72
Palacio del Gobernador (Mérida) 32
Palancar Reef (Cozumel) 15, 53
Palazzo, Cancún 66, 85
Panama hats 75
Pancho's (Mérida) 67
Panuchos 69
Papadzules 69
Paraíso Reef (Cozumel) 15, 52

Parasailing 61
Parque Escultórico Punta Sur (Isla Mujeres) 21
Parque Garrafón (Isla Mujeres) 21, 54
Parque Santa Lucía (Mérida) 33
Parrot fish 53
Paseo de Montejo (Mérida) 33
Passports 120, 121
"Peg-Leg" 39
Personal security 120–121
Petenes (Campeche) 56, 112
Pharmacies 120
Philip II, King 38
Phrase book 142–4
Pickpockets 120
Piracy 21, 39
Pisté 7, 29, 103
  drinking and entertainment 106
  places to eat 107
Platform of the Jaguars and Eagles (Chichén Itzá) 24–5, 30
Playa de Carmen 10, **16–19**, 80
  accommodations 17, 128, 129, 130, 133
  beaches 16, 50, 83
  diving reefs 53
  drinking and entertainment 86
  fishing 61
  itineraries 6, 7, 81
  nightlife 16, 66–7, 85
  places to eat 87
  shopping 84
  Xcaret 6, 7, 17, **18–19**
Playa Delfines (Cancún) 81, 83
Playa Gaviota Azul (Cancún) 83
Playa Mia (Cozumel) 14, 65
Playa Norte (Isla Mujeres) 20, 83
Playa Paraíso 22
Playa San Francisco (Cozumel) 14, 93, 95
Playa Secreto (Isla Mujeres) 20, 83
Playa Sol (Cozumel) 95
Playacar (Playa del Carmen) 16, 82
  accommodations 128
Plaza Mayor (Mérida) 33
Poc-chuc 68
Police 121
Pollo con mole 68
Pollo oriental de Valladolid 68

Post-classic Revival 42
Postal services 122, 123
Press 122, 123
Private homes, staying in 125
Progreso 111
  bars 114
Puchero 68
Puerta de Mar (Campeche) 38
Puerta de Tierra (Campeche) 38
Puerto Aventuras 51, 61, 91
  accommodations 128
  bars 98
  nightlife 97
  places to eat 99
  shopping 96
Puerto Juárez 82
Puerto Morelos 56, 61, 62, 79, 81
  accommodations 128, 129, 132, 133
  beaches and reefs 50, 52, 834
  places to eat 70, 87
Pufferfish 53
Punta Allen (Sian Ka'an) 26, 61, 62, 94
  accommodations 129, 132
Punta Bete 62, 73, 79, 83
  accommodations 129
Punta Laguna 56, 65, 94
Punta Maroma 82
  accommodations 128
Punta Sam 82
Punta Santa Cecilia (Cozumel) 14, 93
Punta Solimán 95, 98
Punta Sur Eco Beach Park (Cozumel) 15, 57, 93
Punta Xamach 95
Puuc cities 37, 44–5
Puuc Hills 37, 111
Pyramids
  Acanceh 49
  Castillo de Kukulcán (Chichén Itzá) 7, 8–9, 28–9, 30, 44
  Great Pyramid (Uxmal) 34, 36
  Nohoch Mul (Cobá) 45, 92
  Pyramid of the Magician (Uxmal) 34, 36, 45, 109

Q

Quesadillas 69
Quinta Avenida (Playa del Carmen) 16

R

Radio 122, 123
Rain forest (Sian Ka'an) 27
Rays 53

Relleno negro 68
Resort hotels 125, 128–9
Restaurants 70–71, 124–5
  Cancún and the North 87
  Central Heartland 107
  Cozumel and the South 99
  menu decoder 144
  West, The 115
Río Lagartos 57, 61, 62, 102, 103
  places to eat 106
  tours 103
Río Secreto 64
Road travel 118

S

Sacbé (white ways) 44, 93
Sacred Cenote (Chichén Itzá) 29, 58
Safety
  personal security 120–121
  travel safety advice 120, 121
Sailing 60
Salbutes 69
Salt 103
Samula Cenote 58, 101
San Felipe 62, 101, 105
  accommodations 131
  places to eat 107
San Gervasio (Cozumel) 15, 45, 91, 93
San Miguel (Cozumel) 14, 91
San Miguel Arcángel (Cozumel) 74
Sandals 75
Santa Clara 104
Santa Elena, accommodations 132
Sayil 37, 44, 110, 111
Sea cucumbers 53
Sea Trek (Xcaret) 18
Seasons 73
Secluded Heaven (Tulum) 22
Self-catering 125
Señor Frog's (Cancún) 66, 86
Sergeant majors 53
Sharks 53
Shopping 124
  Cancún and the North 12, 84
  Central Heartland 105
Sian Ka'an Biosphere Reserve 7, 11, **26–7**, 56, 93
Silverwork 75
Skydiving 61

Sleeping Sharks Cave (Isla Mujeres) 20
Snacks 69, 73
Snappers 53
Sopa de lima 69
Sound and light shows
Chichén Itzá 28
Uxmal 35
South Beach (Tulum) 95
Spanish-era Towns 48-9
Spanish conquistadores 42
Spanish phrase book 142-4
Sports and activities 60-61
Stephens, John Lloyd 110
Street food 69, 73

T

Tacos 69
Tankah 22, 94
accommodations 130
Tankah Natural Park 22
Taxis 119
Taylor, Jason deCaires 12
Teabo 48
Telchac 103
Telephone services 122
Television 122, 123
Temples
Monstermouth 36, 43, 44
Temple of the Centipede (Uxmal) 34
Temple of the Jaguars (Chichén Itzá) 30
Temple of the Seven Dolls (Dzibilchaltún) 44, 74, 110
Temple of the Warriors (Chichén Itzá) 29
Tennis 60
Textiles 84, 113
Theme parks *see* Eco-parks and theme parks
Ticul 49, 111, 112
Tihosuco 104
Time difference 123
Tizimín 48, 74, 103, 104
places to eat 107
Tlaloc 43
Tortas 69
Tour operators 124, 125
Tourism 43
Town Beach (Playa del Carmen) 16
Travel
getting there and around 118-19
safety advice 120, 121

Tríos (troubadours) 33
Travelers with Specific Needs 122
Trips and tours 124, 125
Central Heartlands 105
group discounts 73
see also Itineraries
Tulum 10, **22-3**, 63, 76-7, 91
accommodations 129, 130
bars 98
beaches and reefs 22, 51, 52, 95
itineraries 6, 7, 81
nightlife 66, 97
places to eat 70, 99
Pueblo 20
shopping 96
Site 20, 45, 76-7, 91
Turtle Pools (Xcaret) 18-19
Turtles 53
Tutul Xiu 49
Tzompantli (Chichén Itzá) 30

U

Uaymitún 57, 103
Underground Snorkeling River (Xcaret) 19
Uxmal 11, **34-7**, 64, 109
accommodations 127, 131
carvings **36**
itineraries 7, 111
places to eat 115

V

Valladolid 46, 48, 102, 103
accommodations 131, 133
drinking and entertainment 106
places to eat 107
shopping 105
tours 105
Ventura Park (Cancún) 13, 54, 64, 82
Village fiestas 75
Villas 125
Visas 120, 121
Vision Serpents 43
Visitor information 123

W

Walking 119
Warriors' Columns (Chichén Itzá) 30
Water, drinking 120
Water parks *see* Eco-parks and theme parks
Weather 123

West, The 108-15
A Day in the Puuc Hills 111
drinking and entertainment 114
map 108
places to eat 115
shopping 113
sights 109-12
Wildlife
Crococún Crocodile Park 64, 82
Discover Mexico Park 55
Isla Mujeres 20-21
Punta Sur Eco Beach Park (Cozumel) 15
reef animals 53
reserves 56-7
Sian Ka'an Biosphere Reserve 7, 11, **26-7**, 56, 93
Xaman-Ha Aviary (Playa del Carmen) 17
Xcaret 18-19
Windsurfing 60
Women travelers 120
Women's Beading Cooperative (Isla Mujeres) 20
Wood carvings 75

X

Xaman-Ha Aviary (Playa del Carmen) 17
Xcambó 45, 104
Xcanatún 71
accommodations 127
places to eat 115
Xcaret 17, **18-19**, 55, 64, 81
itineraries 6, 7
Xel-Ha (Tulum) 23, 45, 55, 65, 92
Xel-Ha Site 94
Xlacah Cenote (Dzibilchaltún) 59, 110
Xlapak 37, 45, 73, 111, 112
Xplor 54-5, 80-81
Xpu-Ha 53, 81, 93, 95

Y

Yaxcabá 104
Yaxcopoíl Hacienda 111, 112
Yokdzonot Cenote 104
Yucalpetén 112

Z

Zoo (Xcaret) 18

Acknowledgments

This edition updated by

Contributor Julie Schwietert Collazo
Senior Editors Dipika Dasgupta, Alison McGill
Senior Art Editor Stuti Tiwari
Project Editor Rachel Laidler
Assistant Editor Ilina Choudhary
Manager Picture Research Taiyaba Khatoon
Picture Researcher Administrator Vagisha Pushp
Publishing Assistant Simona Velikova
Jacket Designer Jordan Lambley
Senior Cartographer Subhashree Bharati
Cartography Manager Suresh Kumar
Senior DTP Designer Tanveer Zaidi
Senior Production Editor Jason Little
Senior Production Controller Samantha Cross
Managing Editors Shikha Kulkarni, Beverly Smart, Hollie Teague
Managing Art Editor Sarah Snelling
Senior Managing Art Editor Priyanka Thakur
Art Director Maxine Pedliham
Publishing Director Georgina Dee

DK would like to thank the following for their contribution to the previous editions: Clare Peel, Helen Peters, Nick Rider, Shafik Meghji.

The publisher would like to thank the following for their kind permission to reproduce their photographs:
Key: a-above; b-below/bottom; c-centre; f-far; l-left; r-right; t-top

123RF.com: Franck Camhi 107cra; macmonican 103clb; manganganath 82cl; Borna Mirahmadian 74b.

Alamy Stock Photo: age fotostock / Blaine Harrington 17tl, 55b, 60bl, / Gonzalo Azumendi 7tr, / Jordi Camí 3tl, 76-7, / Stuart Pearce 106clb, / Leonardo Díaz Romero 102cb, all 51b; The Art Archive / Gianni Dagli Orti 36cl, 46ca; Danita Delimont / Julie Eggers 105tr, 111cla, 112tr; Reinhard Dirscherl 22bl; Michael Dwyer 43br; John Elk III 4crb; Robert Fried 27crb; Eddy Galeotti 109b; Nicholas Gill 70br; Granger Historical Picture Archive 31b, 42br, 43tl; 31b; Hugh Hargrave 4t; hemis.fr / Gil Giuglio 72tr; Marshall Ikonography 36bc, 96bl, 73tr, 100tl; imageBROKER / Vision 21 21cr; incamerastock 15tc; Brian Jannsen 22-3; Konstantin Kalishko 38-9; Larry Larsen 64cl; Alain Machet (3) 10cr; Michael DeFreitas Central America 65b, 91cr; John Mitchell 12cl, 32br; Mostardi Photography 37cr; Eric Nathan 15bl; NatureWorld 4cl; Brian Overcast 32ca, 63crb; George Oze 54tr; Stefano Paterna 113c; Pictures Colour Library 11cra; Chuck Place 42cl; PhotoV/ Hisham Ibrahim 85cla; robertharding / Michael DeFreitas 90tl; Grant Rooney 84b; Fedor Selivanov 4cla; Septemberlegs 110cla, 110br; Witold Skrypczak 72br, 101cb, 104b; David South 31cr, 33br, 47crb; Johnny Stockshooter 2tr, 40-1; Topcris 80tl; Jane Tregelles 70t; Ken Welsh 35tc; Andrew Woodley 98cla; Xinhua 12br; Ariadne Van Zandbergen 11c, 33tl.

Alux Restaurant & Lounge: 86cla.

Aqua World: 54cl.

Azul Gallery: 196tc.

Carlos 'n Charlie's: 66b, 97tr.

Casa de Piedra: 115cr.

Casa Denis: 99clb.

Dreamstime.com: Sahar Aga 82br; Agcuesta 73br; Jean-luc Azou 37b, 38cl, 56c; Yulia Belousova 28cla; Florian Blümm 44–5; Flavia Campos 71tr; Salvador Ceja 4b; Rafał Cichawa 34–5; Sorin Colac 28–9; Maciej Czekajewski 56tl; Czuber 67b; Eddygaleotti 3tr, 29tl, 38br, 48tl, 83t, 116–7; Eutoch 79t; Vlad Ghiea 6cl; Richard Gunion 69cla; Pablo Hidalgo 24–5; Irishka777 10clb, 14–5, 16–7, 50cr; Javarman 12–3, 48b; Karlos4kintero 10bl; James Kelley 53br; Kmiragaya 88-89; Patryk Kosmider 16bl; Kravka 7br; Jesús Eloy Ramos Lara 11crb, 11bl, 46b; Lev Levin 23cr; Lucagal 101br; Lunamarina 20br, 20–1, 30tr, 50clb, 68tl; Giulio Mignani 29c; Danilo Mongiello 23tl; Thiago Henrique Neves 80–1; Olga Nosova 92tl; Piotr Pawinski 105c; Boris Philchev 102t; Seaphotoart 52tl, 92b; Siempreverde22 2tl, 8–9; Jo Ann Snover 108tl; Softlightaa 34bl; Jose I. Soto 17cr; stockcreations 69br; Jennifer Stone 75br; Alyaksandr Stzhalkouski 13tl; Subbotina 20clb; Barna Tanko 39cr, 112bl; Slobodan Tomic 35cr; Peter Zaharov 58cl; Suriel Ramirez Zaldivar 68crb.

Evolution Music Inc./Cancun Jazz Festival: 74cr.

Experiencias Xcaret: 18t, 18c, 19bl, 78tl, 81cla; Park / Erik Ruiz 19cr.

FLPA: Minden Pictures / Donald M. Jones 11tl, 27cra, / Pete Oxford 26bl.

Getty Images: Tony Anderson 73cl; Witold Skrypczak 26–7, 49tl; Dallas Stribley 62b.

Conaculta-INAH-MEX: Authorized reproduction by the Instituto Nacional de Antropología e Historia 45cl.

La Chaya Maya: 71l.

La Parrilla: 87bl.

MUSA: Elier Amado Gil / The Stills LifeStyle Agency / Gino Caballero 4cr.

Photoshot: Mahaux Charles 109tr; Frank Fell 10cla; Victor Korchenko 61cl; World Pictures / Stuart Pearce 49tl.

Piedra de Agua Hotel Boutique: RolloDigital2014 114cra.

Robert Harding Picture Library: Michael DeFreitas 14cl, 57cr.

Señor Frog's: Stanly photo 66cl.

Shutterstock.com: Kiev.Victor 1

SuperStock: age fotostock 45tr, 61tr, / Blaine Harrington 6tr, 65cr, 94clb, / Cem Canbay 10crb, / Jan Wlodarczyk 30cl, / Jeff Greenberg 75cl, / Richard Maschmeyer 44cl, 101tr; Luis Javier Sandoval Alvarado 53cl; F1 ONLINE 59tr; Franz Marc Frei 57t; Hemis.fr 79cl; imageBROKER / Katja Kreder 95br; LOOK-foto 52b, 60t; Minden Pictures / Pete Oxford 4clb; Photononstop 59b; Travel Library Limited 51tr; Travel Pictures Ltd 62bl.

Cover

Front and spine: **Shutterstock.com:** Kiev.Victor

Back: **Dreamstime.com:** Byelikova cla, Brian Lasenby tl; **Getty Images/iStock:** http://www.christiane-efe.comundefined undefined tr, Mlenny crb; **Shutterstock.com:** Kiev.Victor b.

Pull out map cover

Shutterstock.com: Kiev.Victor

Commissioned Photography Demetrio Carrasco, Linda Whitwam

All other images are: © Dorling Kindersley. For further information see www.dkimages.com.

Penguin Random House

First edition 2003

Published in Great Britain by
Dorling Kindersley Limited
DK, One Embassy Gardens, 8 Viaduct Gardens, London SW11 7BW, UK

The authorised representative in the EEA is Dorling Kindersley Verlag GmbH. Arnulfstr. 124, 80636 Munich, Germany

Published in the United States by
DK Publishing, 1745 Broadway, 20th Floor, New York, NY 10019, USA

Copyright © 2003, 2023 Dorling Kindersley Limited

A Penguin Random House Company

23 24 25 26 10 9 8 7 6 5 4 3 2 1

A CIP catalog record is available from the British Library.

A catalog record for this book is available from the Library of Congress.

ISSN 1479-344X

ISBN 978-0-2416-2491-3

Printed and bound in Malaysia

www.dk.com

As a guide to abbreviations in visitor information blocks: **Adm** = admission charge; **D** = dinner; **L** = lunch.

MIX
Paper | Supporting responsible forestry
FSC
www.fsc.org
FSC™ C018179

This book was made with Forest Stewardship Council™ certified paper – one small step in DK's commitment to a sustainable future.
**For more information go to
www.dk.com/our-green-pledge**

Phrase Book

In an Emergency

Help!	¡Socorro!	soh-**koh**-roh
	¡Auxilio!	o-xe-leo
Stop!	¡Pare!	**pah**-reh
Call a doctor!	¡Llame a un médico!	yah-**meh** ah **oon** meh-**dee**-koh
Call an ambulance!	¡Llame una ambulancia!	yah-meh ah **oonah** ahm-boo-**lahn**-see-ah
Call the fire department!	¡Llame a los bomberos!	yah-**meh** ah lohs bohm-**beh**-rohs
Police!	¡policía!	poh-lee-**see**-ah

Communication Essentials

Yes	Sí	see
No	No	noh
Please	Por favor	pohr fah-**vohr**
Thank you	Gracias	**grah**-see-ahs
Excuse me	Perdone	pehr-**doh**-neh
Hello	Hola	**oh**-lah
Bye (casual)	Chau	chau
Goodbye	Adiós	ah-dee-**ohs**
What?	¿Qué?	keh
When?	¿Cuándo?	**kwahn**-doh
Why?	¿Por qué?	pohr-**keh**
Where?	¿Dónde?	**dohn**-deh
How are you?	¿Cómo está usted?	**koh**-moh ehs-**tah** oos-**tehd**
Very well, thank you	Muy bien, gracias	mwee bee-**ehn grah**-see-ahs
Pleased to meet you	Mucho gusto	**moo**-choh **goo**-stoh
See you soon	Hasta pronto	**ahs**-tah **prohn**-toh
I'm sorry	Lo siento	loh see-**ehn**-toh

Useful Phrases

That's fine	Está bien	ehs-**tah** bee-**ehn**
Great/fantastic!	¡Qué bien!	keh bee-**ehn**
Where is/are…?	¿Dónde está/están…?	**dohn**-deh ehs-**tah**/ehs-**tahn**
How far is it to…?	¿Cuántos metros/ kilómetros hay de aquí a…?	**kwahn**-tohs **meh**-trohs/ kee-**loh**-meh-trohs **eye** deh ah-**kee** ah
Which way is it to…?	¿Por dónde se va a…?	pohr **dohn**-deh seh **vah** ah
Do you speak English?	¿Habla inglés?	**ah**-blah een-**glehs**
I don't understand	No comprendo/ entiendo	noh kohm-**prehn**-doh
I would like	Quisiera/ Me gustaría	kee-see-**yehr**-ah meh goo-stah-**ree** ah

Useful Words

big	grande	**grahn**-deh
small	pequeño/a	peh-**keh**-nyoh/ nyah
hot	caliente	kah-lee-**ehn**-teh
cold	frío/a	**free**-oh/ah
good	bueno/a	**bweh**-noh/nah
bad	malo/a	**mah**-loh/lah
open	abierto/a	ah-bee-**ehr**-toh/tah
closed	cerrado/da	sehr-**rah**-doh/dah
full	lleno/a	**yeh**-noh/nah
empty	vacío/a	vah-**see**-oh/ah
left	izquierda	ees-key-**ehr**-dah
right	derecha	deh-**reh**-chah
(keep) straight ahead	(siga) derecho	(see-gah) deh-**reh**-choh
near	cerca	**sehr**-kah
far	lejos	**leh**-hohs
more	más	mahs
less	menos	**meh**-nohs
entrance	entrada	ehn-**trah**-dah
exit	salida	sah-**lee**-dah
elevator	el ascensor	ehl ah-sehn-**sohr**
toilets	baños/	**bah**-nyohs/
women's	de damas	deh **dah**-mahs
men's	de caballeros	deh kah-bah-**yeh**-rohs

Post Offices and Banks

Where can I change money?	¿Dónde puedo cambiar dinero?	**dohn**-deh **pweh**-doh kahm-bee-**ahr** dee-**neh**-roh
How much is the postage to…?	¿Cuánto cuesta enviar una carta a…?	**kwahn**-toh **kweh**-stah ehn-vee-**yahr** oo-nah **kahr**-tah ah
I need stamps	Necesito estampillas	neh-seh-**see**-toh ehs-tahm-**pee**-yah

Shopping

How much does this cost?	¿Cuánto cuesta esto?	**kwahn**-toh **kwehs**-tah **ehs**-toh
I would like…	Me gustaría…	meh goos-tah-**ree**-ah
Do you have?	¿Tienen?	tee-**yeh**-nehn
Do you take credit cards/ traveler's checks?	¿Aceptan tarjetas de crédito/ cheques de viajero?	ah-**sehp**-tahn tahr-**heh**-tahs deh **kreh**-dee-toh/ **cheh**-kehs deh vee-ah-**heh**-roh
I am looking for…	Estoy buscando…	ehs-**tohy** boos-**kahn**-doh
expensive	caro	**kahr**-oh
cheap	barato	bah-**rah**-toh
budget friendly	económico	eh-koh-**noh**-mee-koh
white	blanco	**blahn**-koh
black	negro	**neh**-groh
red	rojo	**roh**-hoh
yellow	amarillo	ah-mah-**ree**-yoh
green	verde	**vehr**-deh
blue	azul	ah-**sool**
antique store	la tienda de antigüedades	lah tee-**ehn**-dah deh ahn-tee-gweh-**dah**-dehs
bakery	la panadería	lah pah-nah-deh-**ree**-ah
bank	el banco	ehl **bahn**-koh

bookstore	la librería	lah lee-breh-ree-ah
butcher's	la carnicería	lah kahr-nee-seh-ree-ah
cake store	la pastelería	lah pahs-teh-leh-ree-ah
jeweler's	la joyería	lah hoh-yeh-ree-yah
market	el tianguis/ mercado	ehl tee-ahn-goo-ees/mehr-kah-doh
newsstand	el puesto de periódicos	ehl puh-as-toh deh pe-rio-dee-kohs
post office	la oficina de correos	lah oh-fee-see-nah deh kohr-reh-ohs
shoe store	la zapatería	lah sah-pah-teh-ree-ah
supermarket	el supermercado	ehl soo-pehr-mehr-kah-doh
travel agency	la agencia de viajes	lah ah-hehn-see-ah deh vee-ah-hehs

Transportation

When does the… leave?	¿A qué hora sale el…?	ah keh oh-rah sah-leh ehl dohn-deh
Where is the bus stop?	¿Dónde está la parada de buses?	dohn-deh ehs-tah lah pah-rah-dah deh boo-sehs
Is there a bus/ train to…?	¿Hay un camión/ tren a…?	eye oon kah-mee-ohn/trehn ah…?
platform	el andén	ehl ahn-dehn
ticket office	la taquilla	lah tah-kee-yah
round-trip ticket	un boleto de ida y vuelta	oon boh-leh-toh deh ee-dah ee voo-ehl-tah
one-way ticket	un boleto de ida solamente	oon boh-leh-toh deh ee-dah soh-lah-mehn-teh
airport	el aeropuerto	ehl ah-ehr-oh-poo-ehr-toh

Sightseeing

art gallery	galería de arte	gal-uh-ree-uh deh arh-teh
art museum	el museo de arte	ehl moo-seh-oh deh ahr-teh
beach	la playa	lah plah-yah
cathedral	la catedral	lah kah-teh-drahl
church	la iglesia/ la basílica	lah ee-gleh-see-ah/lah bah-see-lee-kah
garden	el jardín	ehl hahr-deen
museum	el museo	ehl moo-seh-oh
pyramid	la pirámide	lah pee-rah-meed
ruins	las ruinas	lahs roo-ee-nahs
tourist information office	la oficina de turismo	lah oh-fee-see-nah deh too-rees-moh
ticket	la entrada	lah ehn-trah-dah
guide (person)	el/la guía	ehl/lah gee-ah

guide (book)	la guía	lah gee-ah
map	el mapa	ehl mah-pah
taxi stand	sitio de taxis	see-tee-oh deh tahk-sees

Staying in a Hotel

Do you have a vacant room?	¿Tienen una habitación libre?	tee-eh-nehn oo-nah ah-bee-tah-see-ohn lee-breh
double room	habitación doble	ah-bee-tah-see-ohn doh-bleh
single room	habitación sencilla	ah-bee-tah-see-ohn sehn-see-yah
room with a bath	habitación con baño	ah-bee-tah-see-ohn kohn bah-nyoh
shower	la ducha	lah doo-chah
I have a reservation	Tengo una habitación reservada	tehn-goh oo-nah ah-bee-tah-see-ohn reh-sehr-vah-dah
key	la llave	lah yah-veh

Eating Out

Have you got a table for…	¿Tienen mesa para…?	tee-eh-nehn meh-sah pah-rah
I want to reserve a table	Quiero reservar una mesa	kee-eh-roh reh-sehr-vahr oo-nah meh-sah
The bill, please	La cuenta, por favor	lah kwehn-tah pohr fah-vohr
I am a vegetarian	Soy vegetariano/a	soy veh-heh-tah-ree-ah-no/na
waiter/waitress	mesero/a	meh-seh-roh/rah
menu	la carta	lah kahr-tah
wine list	la carta de vinos	lah kahr-tah deh vee-nohs
glass	un vaso	oon vah-soh
bottle	una botella	oo-nah boh-teh-yah
knife	un cuchillo	oon koo-chee-yoh
fork	un tenedor	oon teh-neh-dohr
spoon	una cuchara	oo-nah koo-chah-rah
breakfast	el desayuno	ehl deh-sah-yoo-noh
lunch	la comida	lah koh-mee-dah
dinner	la cena	lah seh-nah
main course	el plato fuerte	ehl plah-toh foo-ehr-teh
starters	las entradas	lahs ehn-trah-das
dish of the day	el plato del día	ehl plah-toh dehl dee-ah
tip	la propina	lah proh-pee-nah
Is service included?	¿El servicio está incluido?	ehl sehr-vee-see-oh ehs-tah een-kloo-ee-doh

Menu Decoder

el aceite	*ah-see-eh-teh*	oil
las aceitunas	*ah-seh-toon-ahs*	olives
el agua mineral	*ah-gwa mee-neh-rahl*	mineral water
sin gas/con gas	*seen gas/kohn gas*	still/sparkling
el ajo	*ah-hoh*	garlic
el arroz	*ahr-rohs*	rice
el azúcar	*ah-soo-kahr*	sugar
una bebida	*beh-bee-dah*	drink
el café	*kah-feh*	coffee
la carne	*kahr-neh*	meat
la cebolla	*seh-boh-yah*	onion
el cerdo	*sehr-doh*	pork
la cerveza	*sehr-veh-sah*	beer
el chocolate	*choh-koh-lah-teh*	chocolate
la ensalada	*ehn-sah-lah-dah*	salad
la fruta	*froo-tah*	fruit
el helado	*eh-lah-doh*	ice cream
el huevo	*oo-eh-voh*	egg
el jugo	*hoo-goh*	juice
la langosta	*lahn-gohs-tah*	lobster
la leche	*leh-cheh*	milk
la mantequilla	*mahn-teh-kee-yah*	butter
la manzana	*mahn-sah-nah*	apple
los mariscos	*mah-rees-kohs*	seafood
la naranja	*nah-rahn-hah*	orange
el pan	*pahn*	bread
las papas	*pah-pahs*	potatoes
el pescado	*pehs-kah-doh*	fish
picante	*pee-kahn-teh*	spicy
la pimienta	*pee-mee-yehn-tah*	pepper
el plátano	*pla-tah-noh*	banana
el pollo	*poh-yoh*	chicken
el postre	*pohs-treh*	dessert
el queso	*keh-soh*	cheese
el refresco	*reh-frehs-koh*	soft drink/soda
la sal	*sahl*	salt
la salsa	*sahl-sah*	sauce
la sopa	*soh-pah*	soup
el té	*teh*	herb tea (usually chamomile)
té negro	*teh neh-groh*	black tea
la torta	*tohr-tah*	sandwich
las tostadas	*tohs-tah-dahs*	toast
el vinagre	*vee-nah-greh*	vinegar
el vino blanco	*vee-noh blahn-koh*	white wine
el vino tinto	*vee-noh teen-toh*	red wine

Numbers

	Spanish	Pronunciation
0	cero	*seh-roh*
1	uno	*oo-noh*
2	dos	*dohs*
3	tres	*trehs*
4	cuatro	*kwa-troh*
5	cinco	*seen-koh*
6	seis	*says*
7	siete	*see-eh-teh*
8	ocho	*oh-choh*
9	nueve	*nweh-veh*
10	diez	*dee-ehs*
11	once	*ohn-seh*
12	doce	*doh-seh*
13	trece	*treh-seh*
14	catorce	*kah-tohr-seh*
15	quince	*keen-seh*
16	dieciséis	*dee-eh-see-seh-ees*
17	diecisiete	*dee-eh-see-see-eh-teh*
18	dieciocho	*dee-eh-see-oh-choh*
19	diecinueve	*dee-eh-see-nweh-veh*
20	veinte	*veh-een-teh*
21	veintiuno	*veh-een-tee-oo-noh*
22	veintidós	*veh-een-tee-dohs*
30	treinta	*treh-een-tah*
31	treinta y uno	*treh-een-tah ee oo-noh*
40	cuarenta	*kwah-rehn-tah*
50	cincuenta	*seen-kwehn-tah*
60	sesenta	*seh-sehn-tah*
70	setenta	*seh-tehn-tah*
80	ochenta	*oh-chehn-tah*
90	noventa	*noh-vehn-tah*
100	cien	*see-ehn*
101	ciento uno	*see-ehn-toh oo-noh*
102	ciento dos	*see-ehn-toh dohs*
200	doscientos	*dohs-see-ehn-tohs*
500	quinientos	*khee-nee-ehn-tohs*
700	setecientos	*seh-teh-see-ehn-tohs*
900	novecientos	*noh-veh-see-ehn-tohs*
1,000	mil	*meel*
1,001	mil uno	*meel oo-noh*

Time

	Spanish	Pronunciation
one minute	un minuto	*oon mee-noo-toh*
one hour	una hora	*oo-nah oh-rah*
half an hour	media hora	*meh-dee-ah oh-rah*
half past one	la una y media	*lah oo-nah ee meh-dee-ah*
Monday	lunes	*loo-nehs*
Tuesday	martes	*mahr-tehs*
Wednesday	miércoles	*mee-ehr-koh-lehs*
Thursday	jueves	*hoo-weh-vehs*
Friday	viernes	*vee-ehr-nehs*
Saturday	sábado	*sah-bah-doh*
Sunday	domingo	*doh-meen-goh*